A Very Present Help

Meditations in Select Psalms

— KEN MARQUIS —

A Very Present Help

Meditations in Select Psalms

— KEN MARQUIS —

Mall Publishing Co.
THE PRINTED WORD THE PLANTED SEED

HIGHLAND PARK, ILLINOIS

Copyright © 2009 Ken Marquis

Printed in the United States of America
Published by:
Mall Publishing Company
641 Homewood Avenue
Highland Park, Illinois 60035
877.203.2453

Cover and Text Design by Marlon B. Villadiego

All rights reserved. No part of this book may be reproduced or transmitted in any form or by any means, graphic, electronic, or mechanical, including photocopying, recording, taping, or by any information storage or retrieval system, without the permission in writing from the publisher.

Unless otherwise identified "Scripture taken from the NEW AMERICAN STANDARD BIBLE ®, Copyright © 1960, 1962, 1963, 1968, 1971, 1972, 1973, 1975, 1977, 1995 by The Lockman Foundation. Used by permission."

"Scripture taken from THE MESSAGE. Copyright © 1993, 1994, 1995, 1996, 2000, 2001, 2002. Used by permission of NavPress Publishing Group."

ISBN: 1-934165-28-X

For licensing / copyright information, for additional copies or for use in specialized settings contact:

Ken Marquis
4532 East Campo Bello Drive
Phoenix, Arizona 85032

TO DARRELL ROBINSON

- A blessing to the Kingdom -

Acknowledgements

Like all endeavors, there are those who assist in helping along the way until the journey is complete. That is so true in the accomplishment of this book.

Thanks to Michele Novelli for editing the manuscript.

A special word of thanks to Harry Schmidt who ultimately saw that this project was achieved.

I would especially like to thank Natalia Bomar, John Crane, Joel Lamb, Darrell Robinson, Steve Sampson, Donnie Talent and my wife, Lyn, for their constant prodding, questioning and words of encouragement. They truly have been the lifters of my head.

Table of Contents

Acknowledgements vii

Foreword xi

Introduction xiii

Available — Psalm 46 1

Questioning — Psalm 13 7

Restored — Psalm 51 19

Forgiveness — Psalm 130 27

Perspective — Psalm 73 35

Discouragement — Psalm 119 49

Prayer — Psalm 143 61

Help — Psalm 146 73

Fear — Psalm 27 87

Assurance — Psalm 9 95

Final Thoughts 103

Foreword

I don't think there is any Christian who has not found strength, solace and comfort from the Psalms. There is no question they have an indescribable way of bringing understanding and hope into our lives.

The Psalms have been a spiritual staple in the lives of so many. They describe not only our frustration with daily events, our questioning of where God is when we can't seem to locate Him, a promise of direction that we need, but most of all an inspiration to worship.

Ken Marquis does a great job in bringing the passion of specific Psalms into a practical and relevant application to each of us. His words bring nourishment to the soul as he breaks down their more specific meaning and passionately unveils insights that the Lord has revealed to him in his own personal experiences.

As he takes us through these specific Psalms verse by verse, it is truly eye-opening and gratifying how to apply these ancient words of old to our daily circumstance. The cares and pressures of life affect all of us. Ken's gentle way of unlocking these truths as he has listened to the Holy Spirit cause a new dimension of hope to spring forth. His own encounters with the Holy Spirit bring a huge grace and understanding.

As I read through this manuscript I was particularly intrigued by the current relevance the Psalms have to my life at any stage, whether in a crisis or just pursuing more intimacy with God. I was also amazed how the Lord brings correction and adjusts our perspective of life's issues through these anointed Scriptures.

I know you will be blessed and your life will be enriched as you experience a whole new appreciation for the Holy Spirit and His comfort and love for you.

Steve Sampson, Author and evangelist.

Introduction

Probably no other book in the Old Testament is read as much as the Psalms. For centuries people have turned to the Psalms for a variety of reasons. The Psalms have provided guidance, counsel and comfort to those in need. The Psalms have helped strengthen one's faith in times of trial and testing. The Psalms have helped in expressing one's gratitude to God in praise and worship.

The Psalms so vividly describe God and His goodness that they have become nourishment for one's hungry spirit. The Psalms so declare God's eternal loving kindness that they are a source of comfort and encouragement for many. The Psalms supply hope; and where there is hope for the future there is strength to live in the present.

The Psalms are real. Real people birthed them. Since they are expressions of real people, they speak to the issues and circumstances of life. They are expressions of the heart. They are cries from the gut. They are expressed questions of the mind. They are statements of the troubled soul. They are shouts of praise. They are declarations of security. They are exclamations of God's faithfulness. The Psalms are expressions generated from living. The Psalms are all these things and more. For these reasons, and many more, people have cherished them.

Like millions before me I, too, have turned to the Psalms for direction, counsel, encouragement, security, assurance, forgiveness, and hope. At times I find they express exactly what I want to say. At other times I have found myself praying the very words of a Psalm. Singing certain Psalms has brought great joy to my heart. I have never been disappointed from my encounter with the contents. So many times the Psalms seem to have been the modem that has allowed me to connect with the presence of God.

In the pages that follow I have shared some Psalms that have spoken specifically to me over the years. I'm not suggesting that other Psalms have not, but these are some that I go back to often. Since there are 150 Psalms to choose from, I'm sure that everyone has their favorites. Besides the universal favorites such as Psalm 1; 23 and 150, the following Psalms are some of my favorites. They are Psalms that address issues of life that we all face.

It is my hope and prayer that these select Psalms will be a *very present help;* that they will speak to you as they have spoken to me; and that you will be blessed and encouraged because of the encounter.

Trust in Him at all times, O people;
Pour out your heart before Him;
God is a refuge for us.
Psalm 62:8

Psalm 46

1. God is our refuge and strength,
   A very present help in trouble.

2. Therefore we will not fear, though the earth should change
   And though the mountains slip into the heart of the sea;

3. Though its waters roar and foam,
   Though the mountains quake at its swelling pride. Selah.

4. There is a river whose streams make glad the city of God,
   The holy dwelling place of the Most High.

5. God is in the midst of her, she will not be moved;
   God will help her when morning dawns.

6. The nations made an uproar, the kingdoms tottered;
   He raised His voice, the earth melted.

7. The Lord of hosts is with us;
   The God of Jacob is our stronghold. Selah.

8. Come, behold the works of the Lord,
   Who has wrought desolations in the earth.

9. He makes wars to cease to the end of the earth;
   He breaks the bow and cuts the spear in two;
   He burns the chariots with fire.

10. "Cease striving and know that I am God;
    I will be exalted among the nations,
    I will Be exalted in the earth."

11. The Lord of hosts is with us;
    The God of Jacob is our stronghold. Selah.

Available

God is our refuge and strength, a very present help in trouble.

- Psalm 46:1

"I can feel for you but I can't reach you." Have you ever had someone say that to you? It is a nice way of saying that they can express sympathy for the situation that you are in, but they can do nothing about it. Have you ever been in a situation where help was needed and assistance was available but not accessible? How frustrating it is to be so close to help and yet it is just beyond reach. I'm fairly confident that all of us have found ourselves in such circumstances, but not with God!

In the first verse of Psalm 46 we are told that God is a very *present help in trouble*. In other words, He is abundantly available for help in tight places. "God is a safe place to hide, ready to help when we need him" (The Message). There is no "I can feel you but can't reach you" with God. There is no looking at the answer to your situation but seeing a closed sign on the door of resolve. There is no near but yet so far away with God. There is just the opposite. The psalmist tells us that God is a very *present help* or is abundantly available for help in the time of need.

Since our God is available for help, we do not need to be afraid or distressed irrespective of the situation before us. His help is available for all circumstances of life, big or small. The events listed in verses two and three of this Psalm are catastrophic.

The earth is changing and the mountains are slipping into the sea. Yet, even if we were to experience such things, we do not have to be afraid because our God is a very *present help* in times of trouble. If we can have peace when such cataclysmic events as these are occurring, we can rest assured that His help is more than sufficient to rectify our situation.

We are also told in this Psalm that God is our refuge and strength. Let's take a look at these two concepts.

First of all, we are told that God is our refuge. As our refuge, He is our place of safety and comfort in times of trouble. He is our safe house. Just like government agencies put people in their protection programs to remove them from danger, God puts us in His protection program to provide comfort and shelter, and to remove us from danger. The nice thing about God's safe house, unlike government safe houses, is that it is totally safe and impenetrable.

Next we are told that He is our strength. Just like ivy has no strength in itself, but takes on the strength of the tree or building it cleaves to, we are told that God is our strength. In other words, as we wrap ourselves around God in faith, allegiance and obedience, we take on His strength.

As a result of God being our refuge and our strength we do

not have to be afraid when unforeseen or unimaginable trouble comes our way. Why? In the time of trouble God is a very *present help*. Regardless of what the trouble is, help is certain because God is *present* with us. The Lord of hosts is with us. Our God who has infinite resources available at His disposal is *present* to assist us. Our covenant God who musters and commands all the hosts of angel armies for our benefit and welfare is with us. The Scripture reminds us, "Isn't it obvious that all angels are sent to help out with those lined up to receive salvation?" (Hebrews 1:14, The Message) Think about it. God has millions of angels at His disposal for our benefit.

Take a moment and think about all the wonderful things that angels have done for God's people throughout Scripture. Consider the times of deliverance, provision and protection that were provided by angels. For example, one angel struck down 185,000 Assyrians and delivered King Hezekiah and the children of God from the King of Assyria (2 Kings 18-19). One angel. According to Revelation 20:1-2, one unnamed angel is going to be able to overpower and bind up the arch enemy of God and Christians for one thousand years. One angel. Then realize that our covenant God, who controls all the angels, is available to assist and help us when we find ourselves in tight places.

That is why we are told to stop striving; let go of that which we cannot alter and relax knowing our covenant God is available to help. He is present. The Lord of hosts is with us. God, who is in control of all the angels, who are present to assist us, is with us.

Our God is our stronghold; a fortified place of refuge. God is a very present help in the time of trouble. He is a very PRESENT (here, near and available) help in the time of trouble. The Lord is a very present HELP (assistance) in the time of trouble. The Almighty is a very present help in the TIME (any minute, hour, day, week and month) of trouble. Our Covenant One is a very present help in the time of TROUBLE (disappointment, frustration, loss and difficulty). Our God is a very PRESENT HELP in the TIME of TROUBLE.

Oh heavenly Father I need Your help.
The situation that I am facing
is beyond my ability and resources to
rectify. Would You invade my life and be a
very present help to me in this time of trouble?
Thank you.

Psalm 13

1. How long, O Lord? Will You forget me forever?
   How long will You hide Your face from me?

2. How long shall I take counsel in my soul,
   Having sorrow in my heart all the day?
   How long will my enemy be exalted over me?

3. Consider and answer me, O Lord my God;
   Enlighten my eyes, or I will sleep the sleep of death,

4. And my enemy will say, "I have overcome Him,"
   And my adversaries will rejoice when I am shaken.

5. But I have trusted in Your loving kindness;
   My heart shall rejoice in Your salvation.

6. I will sing to the Lord,
   Because He has dealt bountifully with me.

Questioning

How long, O Lord? Will You forget me forever?

- Psalm 13: 1

I am confident that most believers are in full agreement with the apostle Paul when he tells us, "Now to Him who is able to do far more abundantly beyond all that we ask or think..." (Ephesians 3:20). Belief in this fact about God is fundamental to one's Christian faith. Nothing is impossible with God is the believer's mantra.

The question that surfaces in most believers' lives is not the "able-ness" of God to alter a situation. The questions that most believers war with are: "Since God is able, *how long* is it going to be until He performs? *How long* until God answers my prayer? *How long* am I going to have to wait? *How long* until God...?" And the *how long* list goes on.

I wish I knew the answer to the *how long* questions, but I do not. I do not know how long until God intervenes on one's behalf. I do know, however, that we are not the first of God's people to ask this question. We are not the first to be perplexed by God's seeming inactivity in our lives. Over 3,000 years ago David found himself in this dilemma of knowing God was able but wondering when God was going to manifest Himself and make a difference in his life.

David's struggle with the *how long* issue can be seen in Psalm 13. This Psalm not only tells us that questions about God will arise in our faith walk, but this Psalm also informs us how to resolve the questioning.

It is important for us to realize that in this Psalm, David is not wrestling with God's ability to perform. What David is warring with is his own doubt as to God's performance in his personal life. This fact should be obvious. If David was questioning God's ability to act he would not be asking God for help. Why pray to a God who is impotent? What David is questioning is God's manifested able-ness in his own circumstances. Without intending to be presumptuous, I think this is the battlefield in which most of us find ourselves. We do not question God's ability but we question His activity in our personal lives.

Think about it. Here is David, who credits God for helping him kill a lion and a bear, who knows that God delivered Goliath into his hand, who has been protected from Saul's aggressive actions, and who has been chosen and anointed as God's agent for his generation, questioning God's activity in his life. If David with all this evidence of God's activity in his life asked God, "How long," I am sure the *how long* question is going to come up in our lives.

Four times in the first two verses of this Psalm David

asked, "How long?" He asked the Lord, "How long am I to be forgotten? How long am I to be abandoned? How long am I to be left to my own thoughts? How long am I to be victimized by my enemies?"

In the first set of *how long* questions David informs us that he feels isolated and abandoned from God's attention. Remember David is not questioning God's sovereign ability to perform. What David is questioning is God's timing of performance in his life. It is as though David is saying to God, "I know that You are able to perform in any situation, but *how long* are You going to withhold Your practical help from me? I feel You have forgotten me. I feel as though You have abandoned me."

I know at times in my life I have felt the same way. Maybe you have too. It is not that God's ability to perform is being questioned, but it seems like He is performing in everybody else's lives. We know intellectually that God has not forgotten our phone number, e-mail address or house address, so to speak, but it seems like He has not returned our call or dropped by in a long time. In those times we feel isolated in the vastness of His omnipresence and forgotten in the magnitude of His omniscience.

In those times of self-conceived abandonment and self-imposed isolation, the only place we feel we have to turn for help and direction is internally. This is exactly what David did. David asks God in verse two how long shall he take counsel in his soul? In other words, how long am I going to be left to self-counsel? How long am I going to be consigned to the turmoil of self-thought? I am presently being consumed by worry and thoughts that torment my soul. David who is tired and frustrated with the present situation of self-counsel asks God when He is going to supply some guidance and counsel.

Again, I am sure that if we have ever felt forgotten by God, that the next step in that falsely assumed position, but heart felt reality, is that we are left to ourselves for guidance. We are left alone in our dilemma. And that position of self-guidance and counsel is rarely a good one. When left to our own thoughts and self-counsel it is amazing how we as humans can fabricate all kinds of threatening scenarios in our minds. These self-conceived scenarios that we live out in our heads rarely materialize into reality. Yet their affect on us is detrimental.

The end result of the false assumptions that God has forgotten us and left us to our own thoughts is that we are doomed for disaster and that our enemy is winning the battle. That is exactly the conclusion that David came to. In verse two, David asks, "How long will my enemy be exalted over me?" In other words, How long is this threat to my well-being going to go on? God, when are You going to intervene and vindicate me?

David was so entangled in his present situation that he was not seeing or thinking clearly. He was being conditioned by his current circumstance instead of letting God's past faithfulness in his life condition the present. At times we all do the same thing. Present circumstances can be so intimidating and threatening that they can cause the reality of the truth to be eroded in our lives. The truth, despite our perception of current circumstances, is that God does not forget us. We must not forget that God is *a very present help* in the time of trouble. God does not leave us to ourselves and God ultimately does not let our enemies triumph over us.

David, even in his state of frustration and confusion over God's seeming absence of activity in his life, chooses to entrust his situation to God. He goes to God in prayer. David moves from complaining and asking how long to prayer. David made a choice. It is a choice that we all can make. We need to realize that regardless of how great the cares and pressures of life, we are still in control of where we will turn for help. The choice is ours to make; not the enemy's. David chose to go to God in prayer.

David asks God to consider and answer him. He is asking God to look intimately, with pleasure, favor and care upon him and his request for help. In a dark time in his life, he asks God to enlighten (brighten) his eyes so he won't sleep the sleep of death. This phrase was a Hebrew idiom for life as opposed to death. David is requesting that God would look upon him with favor and let his eyes be bright to reflect health, vigor and life, as opposed to dim, reflecting despair, discouragement, depression and death.

I think David is also requesting that during these dark times that the eyes of his faith might be enlightened so he might see God's activity in his life. He is saying, even though my physical perception of reality is distorted right now, let my spiritual eye sight be at 20/20 so as to see what I am supposed to see during these dark times.

I had this truth made so real to me a number of years ago. I was living and pastoring in Portland, Oregon. I was going through a tough time in the ministry and was feeling much like David must have felt when he penned this Psalm. I was not questioning God's ability but I was questioning His activity in my life. The "how long God," question dominated my waking hours. My frustration was growing by the day. My wife finally suggested that I go over to the coast and get alone with God and work out this point of tension. So I did.

As evening approached, I decided to sit by the large window in my hotel room and watch the sun go down over the horizon of the Pacific Ocean. It was an absolutely beautiful sight as the light of day was gradually squeezed out by the darkness. As the light was exchanging its dominant place with the now swiftly encroaching darkness, I noticed a star had come out. The longer I watched the process of exchange from light to dark I noticed more stars had come out. It was a direct relationship of nature. The darker it became, the more stars appeared until the whole night sky was filled. As I watched the process of nightfall, I had taken pencil and paper and written down the sequence of a star coming out, noting that more stars had come out as it got darker.

The next afternoon as I was praying and asking God to help me resolve the state of tension I was in, I felt God speak to me. It was though He asked me to go get what I had written the night before about the stars coming out. I did and He asked me to read it. I did. I then felt as though He asked me a really dumb question. I felt that He asked, "Where did the stars come out from? Were they in a cosmic garage?"

Speaking without thinking I replied that they didn't come out from anything or anywhere that they are up there all the time, but you can only see them in the dark. Before He answered me, I realized what I had said. He then drove the point of the questioning home when He asked me, "Then are you saying that some things can only be seen in the dark?" That is what I had just said. Those beautiful stars that are used to navigate and guide travelers, enjoyed by lovers, studied by astronomers, and enjoyed by all mankind can only be seen in the dark. Then I heard Him say, "Why then are you complaining about the dark when some things can only be seen and enjoyed in the dark? If it were daylight all the time just think what you would miss out on."

I will never forget that exchange. It changed my life. And I think that is exactly what David was saying when he prayed that God would enlighten his eyes. He was not only asking God for the assurance of physical life but he was also asking for good spiritual eyesight. He was asking God to allow him to see His activity in his life even when it seemed that it wasn't there. He was asking God to let him see what he needed to see. He was asking God to illuminate the way so he might see the right way to proceed. He was asking God for guidance so he might not do something wrong while in the dark which would allow his enemies to rejoice at his stumbling and allow them to sense victory. A simple and short prayer and yet so insightful.

We have often heard that prayer changes things. And it does. Prayer not only changing things, but it also changes us. Prayer allows us see things in their proper relationship. Prayer changes our perspective or our outlook on life. This short prayer that David prayed is the pivotal point of this Psalm. For even though nothing externally had yet changed, internally David's whole countenance changed. He moved from complaining to declaration.

Instead of asking *how long*, he now declares his trust in God's loving kindness. Instead of asking *how long*, he now expresses joy in God's salvation. Instead of asking *how long,* he now says he will sing unto the Lord. The reason for these newfound expressions is because he recognizes that God has dwelt bountifully with him.

I like the way The Message handles verses five and six. It says, "I've thrown myself headlong into Your arms—I'm celebrating Your rescue. I'm singing at the top of my lungs, I'm so full of answered prayers."

Remember nothing externally had changed, but this short little prayer altered David's whole outlook on things. Prayer will also change our outlook on life. Why? For three reasons.

First, prayer re-orients us. When David was asking God *how long*, he was on the wrong azimuth. He was facing the wrong way. He was seeing things from the wrong point of view. But when he prayed, it re-oriented him so that he was facing the correct way.

The second thing prayer does is it re-focuses us. Just because we are re-oriented, that does not necessarily mean we can see things clearly. Prayer not only lines us up on the correct azimuth, but it makes sure that we are in focus so that we see things clearly.

The third thing prayer does is it re-affirms for us that He is able to perform above our expectations. So prayer points us in the right direction, focuses us so that we can see things clearly, it puts things in perspective, and re-affirms for us that He is able to do exceeding, abundantly beyond all that we ask or think.

So when you find yourself questioning God's activity in your personal life and asking, "how long?", remember some things can only be seen in the dark. Ask the Lord what it is you are to learn or see during this time and say a prayer for guidance. For prayer puts the One who is able to change darkness into light back in perspective in our lives.

O Lord help my eyes of faith see Your hand at work in my life even in the dark times. Let me realize that You have not abandoned me or forgotten me just because it is dark. Help me see what it is I am to see and to never forget that in spite of the external circumstances, You are a faithful God, a very present help, who deals bountifully with His children.

Psalm 51:1-12

1. Be gracious to me, O God,
   according to Your loving kindness;
   According to the greatness of Your compassion
   blot out my transgressions.

2. Wash me thoroughly from my iniquity
   And cleanse me from my sin.

3. For I know my transgressions,
   And my sin is ever before me.

4. Against You, You only, I have sinned
   And done what is evil in Your sight,
   So that You are justified when You speak
   And blameless when You judge.

5. Behold, I was brought forth in iniquity,
   And in sin my mother conceived me.

6. Behold, You desire truth in the innermost being,
   And in the hidden part You will make me know wisdom.

7. Purify me with hyssop, and I shall be clean;
   Wash me, and I shall be whiter than snow.

8. Make me to hear joy and gladness,
   Let the bones which You have broken rejoice.

9. Hide Your face from my sins
   And blot out all my iniquities.

10. Create in me a clean heart, O God
    And renew a steadfast spirit within me.

11. Do not cast me away from Your presence
    And do not take Your Holy Spirit from me.

12. Restore to me the joy of Your salvation
    And sustain me with a willing spirit.

Restored

Wash me thoroughly from my iniquity, and cleanse me from my sin.

- Psalm 51:2

David had sinned. Not only had David committed adultery with Bathsheba but, in his attempt to cover up his transgression, he also indirectly committed the murder of Uriah, Bathsheba's husband. David thought he had ingeniously concealed his sins, but the prophet Nathan, under the direction of God, had exposed them. David now stands exposed before God and in need of forgiveness and restoration. In Psalm 51 David is going to pour out his heart before God and ask to be a recipient of God's restoring forgiveness, mercy and grace.

Most of us have not committed murder. A few may have committed adultery. Probably none have committed both murder and adultery, but all of us have sinned and are in need of forgiveness. Not just from our Adamic sin nature, but from our own personal sins. The Scripture, in Romans 3:23, tell us that all have sinned and measure up short when it comes to God's expectations. We all stand in need of forgiveness. And praise be to God, according to 1 John 1:9, we can be forgiven from all and every sin and be restored.

Psalm 51 is a record of David's petition for forgiveness and there are some great insights and truths about forgiveness in this Psalm that can be included in our prayers for forgiveness. In reality, this Psalm can be prayed word for word as our own prayer for forgiveness. This Psalm does not mention a specific offense, but concentrates on the need and process of forgiveness. At one time or another, all Christians have appealed to God for forgiveness based on the principles taught in this Psalm.

The first thing to be noticed in this Psalm is that David appeals to God's loving kindness and compassion. Since God is a God of loving kindness and compassion, David asks that his sins be washed away. I particularly like The Message's handling of verse two. It says, "scrub away my guilt, soak out my sins in your laundry." Scrub and soak. God's laundry always does a good job of cleaning.

The second thing to be noticed in this Psalm is that David takes full responsibility for his transgressions. He doesn't pass the buck. He doesn't try to excuse his actions away because of extenuating circumstances. He realizes that he alone has sinned and his sin is not hidden but in plain sight of God. He accepts full responsibility for his sin. David also does not trivialize his sin. He realizes that not only had he violated social order, but also, in reality, he had sinned against God.

The third thing to be noticed in this Psalm is David realizes that he has a heart problem. David realizes he has an inner man problem. So in verse ten, David asks God to create in him a clean heart or to create in him a clean inner man.

This request is one of the major truths of this Psalm. David is not asking God to repair or fix his bad heart or inner man. David is not asking God for a heart transplant. No, David is asking God to create for him a new heart or new inner man. The Hebrew word used in this verse for create is "bara", and is the same word used in Genesis 1:1 when it says that God created the heavens and the earth. This is a very interesting word. It does not refer to making something out of existing material. There are other Hebrew words that express the idea of forming, establishing or making out of existing material. However, this Hebrew verb "bara" means to create out of nothing, ex nihilo. Only God can do that!

David is asking God to do for him what he can't do for himself. David may be able to discipline his present heart, inner man, or mend his heart to some altered condition, but he is unable to create a new heart or new inner man. To create out of nothing is reserved for God alone. And David is asking for a brand new heart, a new inner man, not a reconditioned one. What David is asking for is what Paul is going to write about in the New Testament when he says, if a man is in Christ old things are passed away and all things become new (2 Corinthians 5:17). David is asking not only for forgiveness, but for a whole new way thinking and acting. David is asking God to re-wire and re-program him.

Like numerous Christians I have read and prayed Psalm 51 many times. But as I was reading this Psalm from The Message, I received a whole new insight from this prayer of David. Verse ten says, "God, make a fresh start in me, shape a Genesis week from the chaos of my life." Eugene Peterson's phrase, "shape a Genesis week from the chaos of my life" leaped out to me like a beacon.

Immediately I asked myself why Peterson would choose the phrase "shape a Genesis week out of the chaos of my life" to get across the idea of creating a clean heart within David? It soon became very clear to me. According to Genesis 1:1, the earth was formless and void before God began His week of creation. Likewise David, according to Peterson, is saying my life right now is void, formless and full of chaos and I need a creative week in my life. In other words, Lord what You did for the void and formless earth, do for me.

What is a Genesis week? It was a week of new beginnings and the establishment of God's plan. It was a demonstration of God's creative excellence. It was a week when God's will met no resistance. It was a week when all things responded in obedience to His voice. It was a week that produced exactly what God wanted. And David is requesting that the same be done in him. To make such a request is to submit to God's Spirit and be open to whatever He desires to produce in one's life.

What is a Genesis week? If we follow the account of the creative week from Genesis chapter one, we see the following. On day one, light is introduced. That speaks of illumination. On day two, God made the firmament that separated the waters above and below. It is obvious that day two was a day of separation and definition. On day three, dry land appeared from the water below, as well as plants, vegetation and trees. This speaks of foundation, solid ground and the availability of provisions for the maintenance of life. On day four, the solar system is created. This speaks of order and a self-governing system for creation. On day five, the fish and birds are created and given the ability to multiply. This speaks of variety and productivity. On day six, land animals, creeping things and man were created and given the ability to multiply. Again, this speaks of variety and productivity, but it also speaks to the ultimate expression in creation; the fact that man was created in the image of God. On day six, the image of God was manifested. On day seven, God completed His creative work week and rested.

This is what constitutes a Genesis week according to Genesis chapters one and two. So when we ask God for a Genesis week to transpire in our lives, as David did, we are recognizing the need for divine intervention and asking for creative activity to transpire.

It is saying that we will put ourselves in a position of submission to God's abiding presence so as to have some illumination in our lives. It is saying we are tired of walking around in a haze making bad decisions. We are asking God to bring some light into our lives so that we may see and avoid the hidden and unexposed.

To ask for a Genesis week is to ask for some separation and definition in our lives for it seems as though everything just runs together.

To ask for a Genesis week is to ask for some foundation and provision in our lives.

To ask for a Genesis week is to request some order and self-discipline in our lives.

To ask for a Genesis week is to ask for variety and productivity to be active in our lives.

To ask for a Genesis week is to desire the image of God to be manifested in our lives.

To ask for a Genesis week is to ask for some rest, peace and completion to come into our lives.

These blessings of creation are available to us today just as they were available to David. They are available to us the same way the first Genesis week happened. If we were to reduce the creation account down to one statement we could say that the Genesis week of creation was a record of obedient responses to God's design, desire and Word. Therefore, if we want a Genesis week in our lives we need to submit to the creative power of His design and desire for our lives and His creative Word.

When we find ourselves in a destitute, sinful or chaotic state we need to ask God to do for us what we cannot do for ourselves. We need to ask God for a Genesis week in our lives.

Father, I realize and recognize that I have sinned, and I am asking You to be a very present help and forgive me. Let me be bathed in Your mercy and grace. Look at me through Your eyes of loving kindness and restore to me the peace of heart and mind that I am okay with You. Create within me a new heart that I might honor You in all that I do. Thank you!

Psalm 130

1. Out of the depths I have cried to You, O Lord.

2. Lord, hear my voice!
   Let Your ears be attentive
   To the voice of my supplications.

3. If You, Lord, should mark iniquities,
   O Lord, who could stand?

4. But there is forgiveness with You,
   That You may be feared.

5. I wait for the Lord, my soul does wait,
   And in His word I do hope.

6. My soul waits for the Lord,
   More than the watchmen for the morning,
   Indeed, more than the watchmen for the morning.

7. O Israel, hope in the Lord;
   For with the Lord there is loving kindness,
   And with Him is abundant redemption.

8. And He will redeem Israel
   From all his iniquities.

Forgiveness

If You, Lord, should mark iniquities, O Lord, who could stand?
But there is forgiveness with You.

- Psalm 130:3-4

I am so thankful that God doesn't keep score of my short comings and sins, but instead, as verse four of this Psalm tells us, God forgives. And Psalm 86:5 tells us that God is good and ready to forgive all who ask.

What is true of God, however, is not always true of man. Whereas God forgives and forgets, man tends not to forgive and remembers. Whereas God does not keep score man tends to keep score. Man is very good at score keeping, and feels justified in so doing. Many times we feel it is our duty to keep personal infractions alive and well in the score books of our minds. Forgiveness is out of the question. Once the infraction is recorded in the score book of the mind, the infringement cannot be erased. We become vaults harboring infectious iniquities, and wonder why we are not well physically, emotionally and/or spiritually. Lack of forgiveness only affects the one keeping score and has little impact on the one that caused the infringement.

There is an old proverb that is so true. It says, "If you are going to function in vengeance, dig two graves." Simply stated, the lack of forgiveness will kill you. Maybe the lack of forgiveness will not kill you physically but it will probably kill you emotionally and will definitely kill you spiritually. How so?

We are told in the Psalm 66:18 that, "If I regard wickedness in my heart, the Lord will not hear." And, at the conclusion of what we know as the Lord's Prayer in Matthew's gospel, Jesus says, "For if you forgive others for their transgressions, your heavenly Father will also forgive you. But if you do not forgive others, then your Father will not forgive your transgressions" (Matthew 6:14-15). Jesus' words make it rather clear that our forgiveness from God is contingent on our offering forgiveness to others. Simply put, if we don't forgive, Jesus doesn't forgive. And if He does not forgive, we are dead in our trespasses or spiritually dead.

These are harsh words but true. These scriptures inform us of the consequences if we refuse to forgive and continue to think we are justified in our scorekeeping. These may be harsh words but we need to hear and apply them.

I am reminded of a story a pastor told me. He was serving the Lord's Supper to a shut-in one day. During the process of serving the emblems, a certain individual's name came up in the discussion. The person receiving the communion said that they would never forgive this person for what they had done. My pastor friend quickly responded by telling the recipient of the sacraments that the person they refused to forgive had been dead for a number of years.

Talk about scorekeeping! This goes beyond scorekeeping and is more like polishing the score book after the game is over. There was no value in serving the Lord's Supper which represents, in emblematic form, Christ's sacrificial act of forgiveness. Here they were, holding the emblems of forgiveness and new life, and at the same time the recipient of the Supper was neutralizing the meaning and value of the emblems with the germs of unforgiveness.

Sometimes the help we need can be found in the act of forgiving. So many times the remedy to the situation that we find ourselves in is just to offer forgiveness. The reason it seems so hard to do is because we feel like we are giving in and releasing any opportunity to get even. However, not offering forgiveness is not aiding the cause, but only prolonging the offense. If you don't forgive, what are you going to do with that hurt you are holding on to? Jesus says, "... If you don't forgive sins, what are you going to with them?" (John 20:23, The Message)

The beauty of forgiveness is that it releases us from the past. Forgiveness offered breaks the rope that ties us to the past. Forgiveness offered allows us to live in the present and anticipate the future without the shackles of the past. If we don't forgive, not only are we bound to the past, but each time we rehearse the past infraction it gets bigger in our minds. The past hurts become like a fish story. The fish (the hurt), gets bigger with each telling.

Lack of forgiveness is like a broken record or scratched disk in your soul that can't move on but plays the infraction over and over. Each time it replays, it produces new pangs of hurt and injustice. Forgiveness is the switch that turns off the playback machine of the memory.

Just because you can remember an incident doesn't mean you haven't forgiven. Of course you are going to remember. The memory is going to be there, but the associated hurt and anger will be gone.

I can still remember the incident that really hurt me. My character and integrity had been attacked. I was angry and hurt. I felt that I had been unjustly treated. It only took a few words and pressing of the correct combination of memory buttons and I would spew forth like an erupting volcano. It took very little to get me talking about my self-perceived, justified hurt. Then one day, about two years later, I found myself thanking God for the hurtful experience and what I had learned. Oh, I still can remember the incident. I can't deny it happened, but the memory of it no longer punches my buttons. I am no longer tied to that event in my life. I can live in the present without that burdensome encumbrance from the past. Why? Because I forgave. And when you forgive, it releases you from the past and brings fairness to the situation. Forgiveness is the great equalizer because it puts a halt to the feelings of unfairness.

How does one forgive? The same way one is forgiven. Forgiveness is offered. It doesn't matter if it is received - it only matters that it is given. Jesus has offered forgiveness to all mankind, but all mankind has not and will not accept His offer. Just because some refuse His offer of forgiveness does not nullify the offer to those that accept it. The key is to set yourself free from the bondage of the past by offering forgiveness.

It is true that we may have been hurt, but why should we

continue to hurt ourselves by not offering to forgive? We are only deceiving ourselves if we think we are getting even with the offender if we don't forgive. In reality we are only causing are own self-inflicted demise.

If we refuse to forgive we are only removing ourselves from the Lord who is good and ready to forgive. If God does not keep score of my shortcomings but offers forgiveness, then why should I keep score for Him by refusing to forgive?

Let us not forget the words of the psalmist:

"If you, God, keep records on wrongdoings, who would stand a chance? As it turns out, forgiveness is your habit, and that's why you're worshiped."

Psalm 130:3-4, The Message

Let us not forget the words of Jesus:

"... You can't get forgiveness from God, for instance, without also forgiving others. If you refuse to do your part, you cut yourself off from God's part."

Matthew 6:14-15, The Message

"If you don't forgive sins, what are you going to do with them?"

John 20:23, The Message

Lord, please teach me to forgive others as
You have forgiven me. Amen

Psalm 73

1. Surely God is good to Israel,
   To those who are pure in heart!

2. But as for me, my feet came close to stumbling;
   My steps had almost slipped.

3. For I was envious of the arrogant,
   As I saw the prosperity of the wicked.

4. For there is no pains in their death;
   And their body is fat.

5. They are not in trouble as other men,
   Nor are they plagued like mankind.

6. Therefore pride is their necklace;
   The garment of violence covers them.

7. Their eye bulges from fatness;
   The imaginations of their heart run riot.

8. They mock and wickedly speak of oppression;
   They speak from on high.

9. They have set their mouth against the heavens,
   And their tongue parades through the earth.

10. Therefore his people return to this place,
    And waters of abundance are drunk by them.

11. They say, "How does God know?
    And is there knowledge with the Most High?"

12. Behold, these are the wicked;
    And always at ease, they have increases in wealth.

13. Surely in vain I have kept my heart pure,
    And washed my hands in innocence;

14. For I have been stricken all day long
    And chastened every morning.

15. If I had said, "I will speak thus,"
    Behold, I would have betrayed
    The generation of Your children.

16. When I pondered to understand this,
    It was troublesome in my sight

17. Until I came into the sanctuary of God;
    Then I perceived their end.

18. Surely You have set them in slippery places;
    You cast them down to destruction.

19. How they are destroyed in a moment!
    They are utterly swept away by sudden terrors!

20. Like a dream when one awakes,
    O Lord, when aroused, You will despise their form.

21. When my heart was embittered,
    And I was pierced within,

22. Then I was senseless and ignorant;
    I was like a beast before You.

23. Nevertheless I am continually with You;
    You have taken hold of my right hand.

24. With Your counsel You will guide me,
And afterward receive me to glory.

25. Whom have I in heaven but You?
And besides You, I desire nothing on earth.

26. My flesh and my heart may fail,
But God is the strength of my
heart and my portion forever.

27. For, behold, those who are far
from You will parish;
You hast destroyed all those
who are unfaithful to You.

28. But as for me, the nearness of God is my good;
I have made the Lord God my refuge,
That I may tell of all Your works.

Perspective

Until I came into the sanctuary of God; Then I perceived their end.
- Psalm 73:17

One of the great challenges of life is the ability to keep everything in its proper relationship. It takes constant attentiveness to keep things in perspective. It is amazing how fast everything gets out of proportional relationship when perspective is lost. Psalm 73 helps us with this ever-present task of keeping everything in life in its proper proportional relationship. It is a Psalm that teaches us how to keep things in perspective.

One of the things that causes perspective to be lost is when we see godly people suffer and ungodly people prosper. One of the great enigmas of life is why do bad things happen to godly people and why do good things happen to people who could care less about God? Psalm 73 provides some insight to this dilemma that will help us in the struggle to keep everything in perspective. In his book, *Out of the Depths*, Bernhard Anderson writes, "Psalm 73 ... grapples with this problem at the profoundest level... ."

What is the problem? Perspective.

I discovered the magnificent truths of Psalm 73 many years ago and it has been a constant blessing to me every since. Over the years, I have often turned to this Psalm for encouragement, reassurance, and, most of all, for adjustment of my perspective on life.

All of us function with a set of core beliefs or presuppositions. These core beliefs or presuppositions are the threads that are used to weave the fabric of our belief system. This belief system, once woven, becomes the grid through which we evaluate all of life. As long as what we see and hear corresponds with what we believe, everything is okay. When observable and audible facts no longer correspond with our foundational belief system, there is gridlock in the belief system. One result of belief system gridlock is the loss of perspective, or at least the clouding of perspective.

This is exactly what happens to the psalmist in this Psalm. In verse one the psalmist makes a bold declaration. He declares, "Surely God is good to Israel, to those who are pure in heart!" This declaration was a core belief for the psalmist. This declaration was a foundational principle by which the psalmist guided his life. But in verses two through three, the psalmist tells us he almost stumbled and slipped. He was caught in belief system gridlock. Why? Because what he saw did not correspond with what he believed. What the psalmist saw was the prosperity of the wicked. What the psalmist believed was God was good to the pure in heart. If what he believed was true, the wicked should not prosper and the righteous should prosper. This scenario was not what he was experiencing. He was observing just the opposite of what he held to be true.

His declaration that God was good to those who were pure in heart was being challenged by observable facts. What he saw that caused him so much distress is found in verses four through twelve. What he saw was well off, arrogant individuals, who seemingly lived out their lives without any restraints, and yet they were better off than those individuals who tried to live by society's rules and honored the desires of God.

The discrepancy between the belief that God is good to Israel (to those who are pure in heart) and the apparent contradictory evidence all around him, almost caused him to stumble, to lose perspective. What he saw had such an impact on him that he was ready to throw in the towel. What he saw almost caused him to abandon his belief system. According to verses thirteen and fourteen the psalmist was persuaded that allegiance to his core beliefs had been a waste of time and had caused him great loss, pain and suffering.

To further compound the issue, according to verses fifteen and sixteen, he feels guilty for feeling this way. He feels like he is betraying all those who had gone on before him who had kept the faith in their core beliefs, notwithstanding the observable contradictory evidence. And yet the more he tries to reconcile the discrepancy between what he sees and what he believes, the more frustrated he becomes.

The psalmist was in a state of despair and frustration. He was suffering from a loss of perspective brought on by conflict between what he believed and what he saw. When perspective is lost, as it was in his situation, it is impossible to see clearly and navigate around the obstacles of life.

Today we face the same dilemma the psalmist faced. Christian life is based on faith in a set of facts that are believed to be true. Just like the psalmist, we, too, have a "cloud of witnesses" that have gone before us and have kept the faith even when what they observed contradicted what they believed. And yet with all the evidence available to us that what we believe is true, it is so easy to lose perspective because what we see does not correspond with what we believe.

As one who has been a believer for many years, I must admit that what I have seen and experienced compared to what I believe is true, often taxes my faith to the max. Just like the psalmist, we know that God is good to those who follow after Him, but sometimes the inequalities in life, seem to put what we know in conflict with what we see.

For example, the modern equivalent to verses four through twelve would be like the guy that cheats on his income tax returns and pilfers things at work but is seemingly never caught. As a result of his actions, he has all kinds of adult toys. You, on the other hand, are honest in your financial dealings and faithfully pay your tithes. You have no adult toys and just seem to get by from paycheck to paycheck. Or, maybe you see the guy next door who spends absolutely no time with his kids and yet they are the nicest kids and honor students at school. You, on the other hand, spend all kinds of time with your children, coach their soccer team and teach Sunday school at your church. Instead of your kids being grateful and model children, they are rebellious and about to flunk out of school.

Perspective

Sometimes the difference between what you know to be true and what you see is so apparent that you feel exactly like the psalmist when he says that it has been a waste of time keeping the heart pure and the hands clean. At times you feel like you live on the street with all the people described in verses four through twelve. You find yourself asking, "What have I done wrong?"

You know what you are feeling is wrong, but you cannot help it. You try to resolve the dilemma by reason, but you cannot. If you are not careful your present condition begins to color everything you say and do. What is so dangerous about this condition of lost perspective is that it feeds upon itself and causes you to be removed further away from the strategic vantage point that can solve the problem of lost perspective.

Our perspective is lost when we are removed from the strategic vantage point that allows us to see things in their proper proportional relationship. Perspective is regained when we are reestablished in that strategic vantage point so as to see things clearly. This is why verse seventeen of this Psalm is so important. It is the pivotal verse in this Psalm, acting as a fulcrum for the rest of the Psalm. This verse tells us how to regain and maintain our perspective. It is the verse that reaffirms our belief system, puts everything back in focus and reestablishes us to a strategic vantage point. It is in the sanctuary of God that the things of life begin to make sense. Until we enter His presence, nothing in this life will ultimately make sense.

When perspective is reestablished, the clarity and validity of the facts will correctly interpret the situations before us instead of the situations incorrectly interpreting the facts. The truth is, God is good to the pure in heart.

It is quite obvious from this Psalm that the psalmist's problem originated from the fact that he mentally, emotionally and/or physically removed himself from the things of the Lord. If he came into the sanctuary he must have been out of the sanctuary. He became consumed with the horizontal cares of life instead of focusing on the vertical source of life. When he again began to interface with the things of the Lord, his dilemma was resolved. For in the sanctuary, in God's presence, he saw the end of the arrogant and wicked. In other words, he saw how temporal and fragile their positions and possessions were. Everything that they possessed could be gone in a fraction of a second. By seeing their end he also saw his end. He saw that what seemed so tantalizing and desirable was temporary at best. The psalmist, when in the sanctuary, in God's presence, realized his benefits. He saw who really had it made.

What does it mean to come into the sanctuary? How does one come into the sanctuary? I think it means to view life from God's perspective as much as it is humanly possible.

My need for reading glasses has helped me understand this idea of coming into His sanctuary. Without my reading glasses I can clearly see things in the distance, but things up close are blurry and out of focus. With my reading glass on, I can see things clearly that are up close but things in the distance are fuzzy and out of focus. Without my glasses I cannot read God's Word, but I can view things in the distance just fine. When I put on my reading glasses the Word of God becomes clear and everything in the distance becomes fuzzy and out of focus. It is everything in the distance that causes me problems and causes me to lose perspective. But when I come into my glasses (put them on) the things in the distance, which caused me to lose perspective, become fuzzy. That which can alter my circumstances, the Word of God, becomes clear.

Coming into the sanctuary means coming into His presence. Coming into the sanctuary means coming into His Word. Coming into the sanctuary means maintaining constant fellowship with Him. Coming into the sanctuary is the practicing of the words of the old chorus:

> *Turn your eyes upon Jesus*
> *Look full in His wonderful face*
> *And the things of earth will grow strangely dim*
> *In the light of His glory and grace.*
> Helen H. Lemmel, 1922

Notice the words of the chorus do not say problems go away. It does say, however, they grow strangely dim. In other words, they lose their impact and influence when put in the backdrop of His presence.

Nothing physically changed around the psalmist. The well-off wicked were still present. The fat cats that disregarded God were still flaunting their resources. Everything was still the same except the psalmist's perspective on the reality of life changed. He had come into the sanctuary.

Now that the psalmist is once again in the sanctuary, he is able to make claims that he was unable to make when not in the sanctuary.

1. He is now aware of God's ever abiding presence and His ever-present right hand (verse 23).

2. He is now conscience of God's gentle, guiding way and that he has a future hope that after his death he will be united with God (verse 24).
3. He now desires nothing on earth. His desire is only for God. Before he came into the sanctuary it was his desire for the things of earth that caused him to lose perspective (verse 25).
4. He now has come to the conclusion that even though his health may fail, God is his strength and his forever (verse 26).
5. Once his perspective was readjusted he has come to the realization that the nearness of God is the best thing he has going for himself. The truth of the matter is God was near all the time, he just did not realize it (verse 28).

I believe that being in the sanctuary is much like the truth taught in Psalm 16:11, "...In Your presence is fullness of joy; In Your right hand there are pleasures forever."

As I mentioned at the beginning of this chapter, Psalm 73 has been a great blessing to me over the years. The truths incorporated in this Psalm speak to many of the situations of life that seem to have no answer. I have shared the truths from this Psalm many times not only with myself, but from the pulpit and in personal counseling. Each and every time I have shared it's truths, it may not have provided specific answers to the looming questions or solved a pending problem, but it has brought rest, assurance, and peace that God is in control. The truths found in Psalm 73 help reestablish perspective in our lives so we can see things clearly and in proper proportional relationship.

It is easy to let the encounters and situations of life wear us down and cause us to become distracted and discouraged. It is easy to have our focus jarred and lose perspective. I honestly do not know how many times I have turned and read Psalm 73 to adjust my focus so I could see clearly what really matters in life, and to have the great truths about God reaffirmed in my spirit.

We need to be reminded that, "...God is the strength of my heart and my portion forever" (verse 26). We need to be reminded that, "...the nearness of God is my good" (verse 28). We need to remember that it is only in the sanctuary of God that the dilemmas and inequalities of life will begin to make any sense and that perspective is gained and maintained.

Lord, help me remember that You are truly good to me all the time. You are my good, and You are truly good to those who are pure in heart.

Psalm 119:81-88

81. My soul languishes for Your salvation;
    I wait for Your word.

82. My eyes fail with longing for Your word,
    While I say, "When will You comfort me?"

83. Though I have become like a wineskin in
    The smoke, I do not forget Your statues,

84. How many are the days of Your servant?
    When will You execute judgment on those
    who persecute me?

85. The arrogant have dug pits for me,
    Men who are not in accord with Your law.

86. All Your commandments are faithful;
    They have persecuted me with a lie;
    help me!

87. They almost destroyed me on earth.
    But as for me, I did not forsake Your precepts.

88. Revive me according to Your loving kindness,
    So that I may keep the testimony of Your mouth.

Discouragement - Burn Out

*Revive me according to Your loving kindness,
so that I may keep the testimony of Your mouth.*
- Psalm 119:88

Burn out. If you haven't experienced it, you probably know someone who has. If not, I'm sure you are at least familiar with the term. Burn out is the term that describes a condition of complete mental and/or physical exhaustion. A condition that incapacitates so that one is not able to function up to par.

In Psalm 119:81-88 the psalmist is declaring that he is burned out, and is asking God to revive him. He does not use our modern day expression "burned out" to describe his condition, but uses a phrase of his day that describes a burned out condition. In verse eighty-three he says that he has become like a "wineskin in the smoke". For our twenty-first century ears this expression may seem a little strange, but to a person living at that time, it made perfect sense.

For in that time, they would hang their wineskins from the roof poles of their tents or the exposed roof beams of their houses. And, as you know, an open fire was used in the tents and houses for heat and cooking. The smoke and soot from the fires would dry out the wineskins and turn them black. As a result of the exposure to the fire and smoke, the wineskins were no longer soft, pliable and useful. Thus the origin of the phrase "I have become like a wineskin in the smoke."

So what the psalmist is saying is, "I feel as though I have served my purpose. I am no longer useful. I am worn out. I am totally exhausted. The exposure to the weight and cares of life has ruined me. I can no longer function for that which I was created. I no longer have purpose. I am just a wineskin in the smoke."

Instead of saying, "I feel like a wineskin in the smoke," we would say, "I am burned out. I am dry. I have not had a creative thought in weeks. I feel like I am on overload. I am mentally and physically exhausted."

Regardless of the phrase that is used, the psalmist is describing the condition that we know as burned out. But while he is in this self-declared condition, I want you to notice what he says. Even though he is distraught and feels totally useless, he says that he will not forget God's statues or Word.

Why is this declaration so important? It is important because his self-diagnosis is based on his external condition caused by smoke. By his declaration, he is declaring that he will not forget God's Word and allow it to be contaminated by the smoke. God's Word is in his inner man where the smoke does not penetrate. So even though the external circumstances may dictate his perceived external condition, the psalmist realizes that his only hope of recovery is attentiveness to the deposit of God's Word in his inner man.

Have you ever cooked over a campfire? The pan, or pot, that is being used is blackened by the fire and smoke. No matter how black the outside of the pan or pot gets, the smoke does not affect the contents of the pot, which are clean and nourishing. I believe the psalmist is saying that no matter what the external evidence says, or how I feel at the moment, I will not forget what is in the pot. No matter how black things seem to be on the outside, I will not forget what is on the inside. I will not forget God's Word.

When the psalmist says that he will not forget, he is not talking about a temporary or permanent lapse of memory. Rather he is talking about an activity that has been prompted by intent.

To forget can mean to ignore. To ignore something is to be aware of its presence, but intentionally pay no attention to it.

To forget can also convey the idea that one will abandon currently held truths and follow after other ideas, teachings and philosophies. Therefore, to forget can mean to vacillate in preferences.

To forget can also mean to offer up a challenge or not to follow prescribed counsel. It means to go one's way and not to wait. Psalm 106:13 is an example of this attitude. The psalmist, speaking about the children of Israel, says, "They quickly forgot His works; They did not wait for His counsel."

So the psalmist is saying that no matter how he feels or looks on the outside he will not forget God's Word. He will not ignore God's Word. He will not abandon God's Word. He will not challenge God's Word. Instead he will do just the opposite. According to verse eighty-one, he will wait for God's Word or hope in God's Word. In other words, he is going to hang on to God's Word with all his strength and consciousness. He believes his attachment to God's Word is the answer to his burned out condition.

To wait or hope in God's Word is not a static condition. The psalmist does not say he is going to wish for God's Word. Wishing is just a mental activity between the ears. He says that he is going to wait for, or hope in, God's Word. Hoping is dynamic. Hope is living with expectation. Hope is forward-looking. Hope springs forth from the inside of man and affects the outside. Hope can change the condition of wineskins. Hope says tomorrow and the future can be different from the cares, frustrations and problems of today. Hope says things can and will be different. It is hope in the future that provides strength and courage to live in the present.

Hope is the engine that moves us on and upward on the road of life, but like all engines, hope needs fuel to run. The Bible is real plain about where our fuel comes from. The Scripture tells us, "…man does not live by bread alone, but man lives by everything that proceeds out of the mouth of the Lord" (Deuteronomy 8:3). The fuel for our engine of hope is the high-octane Word of God. It is God's Word that keeps our engine of hope running. God's Word is our fuel source.

So even though the psalmist declares how he feels (like a wine skin in the smoke) he also makes some declarations of intent. Even though he feels one way, he will not let his perceived condition alter his life style. Look what he declares:

In verse 81, he tells us that he will wait or hope for God's Word.

In verse 83, he tells us that he will not forget God's Word.

In verse 87, he tells us that he will not forsake God's Word.

Even though the external circumstance of life have so affected him that he no longer feels useful or that he can fulfill his created function, he says that he will not abandon God's Word. Even though the cares of life have worn him down so that he is mentally and physically exhausted, he says that he will continue to wait on or hope in God's Word. Even though he feels like a wine skin in the smoke or is burned out, he says he will not forget God's Word.

Why? Because the psalmist believes that God can revive and recondition him so that what is in his heart - God's Word - may ultimately be in his mouth (Verse 88). The psalmist believes that the Word of God can change him from the inside out. So instead of being a wineskin in the smoke, the psalmist believes he can become an instrument of praise if he does not abandon God's Word. Why? Because God's Word is a powerful change agent.

What can we learn from this Psalm that will help us in our times of discouragement, despair and burn out?

First of all, we need to know that trust in God's Word will change our nature and then our self-concept. The apostle Peter tells us, "... you have been born again not of seed which is perishable but imperishable, that is, through the living and enduring Word of God" (1 Peter 1:23). The living and abiding Word of God is the agent of change. Paul tells us that "... if anyone is in Christ, he is a new creature; the old things have passed away; behold, new things have come" (2 Corinthians 5:17). God's Word will change our self-concept because when we believe His Word, it changes us. I could go on and on about the importance of God's Word, but suffice to say, from the first chapter of Genesis to the last chapter of Revelation, attentiveness and obedience to God's Word is the means to change, preservation and blessing.

Second, we need to realize that trust in God's Word will change our perspective on life. God's Word will not only change our self-concept, but it will change how we perceive the world in which we live. God's Word will allow us to realize that we are in relationship with the One who made the world and all that is in it. God's Word will allow us to see that He is able and in absolute control. God's Word will inform us that we are in the hands of the One who holds the world in His hands. We need to learn to look at the world that we live in through His hands and not our circumstances.

The prophet, Jeremiah, was aware of the value of God's Word affecting one's perspective of the world. Jeremiah had the ability to see the world through God's Word instead of present conditions. In a very difficult time for the southern nation of Judea, God's Word altered Jeremiah's perspective. When the armies of Babylon were besieging Jerusalem, God told Jeremiah to buy some land. It doesn't take a rocket scientist to know that when your nation is about to be conquered, it is not the best time to buy land. Leaving aside the current political conditions, Jeremiah obeyed God's directive and bought the land. Since Jeremiah was obedient to God's Word, the Lord spoke to him words of assurance (Jeremiah 32:15) that caused Jeremiah to proclaim this great statement of perspective.

> Ah Lord God! Behold, You have made the heavens and the earth by Your great power and Your outstretched arm! Nothing is too difficult for You... (Jeremiah 32:17).

God, Himself, made a similar declaration when He told Abraham and Sarah that they would have a child the following year. Their current perspective on life, their knowledge and facts pertaining to procreation, said that it was impossible. Sarah was an old woman past childbearing years. But God said, "Is anything too difficult for the Lord?..." (Genesis 18:14) Belief and trust in God's Word changed their perspective on life and Isaac was born.

Jesus also makes a similar declaration about God's ability when He is explaining to the disciples how difficult it is for a rich man to enter the kingdom of heaven. The disciples in response to His teaching asked, "Who can be saved?" Jesus responds to their question by saying, "With people this is impossible, but with God all things are possible" (Matthew 19:26).

The apostle Paul sums up the fact that God's Word, when believed, can alter one's concept or perspective on life when he says, "Now to Him who is able to do far more abundantly beyond all that we ask or think, according to the power that works within us..." (Ephesians 3:20).

Considering these scriptures, we need to take to heart and practice Jesus' teaching in Matthew chapter six when he tells us not to be anxious about the concerns of life and to be more concerned about the kingdom of God. We need to let God's Word form our perspective on life instead of current events or circumstances.

Third, we need to know that God's Word can and does set us free. It releases us from the past. God's Word is emancipating.

Jesus tells us, "If you continue in My Word, then you are truly disciples of Mine; and you will know the truth, and the truth will make you free" (John 8:31-32). The word translated "free" can also mean to liberate or deliver. God's Word is truth and, therefore, can free us from sin and the guilt of the past. The psalmist in Psalm 119 tells us that God's Word is truth (verse 142), that all God's Word is truth (verse 151), and that the sum of God's Word is truth (verse160). God's Word, the truth, is the agent of freedom, liberation, deliverance, and emancipation.

No wonder the psalmist says that he will not forget God's Word. It is God's Word that is going to free him from his self-evaluation of being a dried up wineskin in the smoke.

Fourth, we need to know that God's Word also provides comfort. In times of stress, anxiety, fear, grief, or whatever emotionally taxing state one is in, God's Word can and does provide relief and comfort. His Word is a *very present help* in all situations.

There are too many scriptures that speak about God's Word providing relief and comfort to reference them all. A few scriptures that speak of God's ever-present help and that provide comfort in specific areas of need are:

Strength – "Do not fear, for I am with you; Do not anxiously look about you, for I am your God. I will strengthen you, surely I will help you, surely I will uphold you with My righteous right hand" (Isaiah 41:10).

Provision – "The young lions do lack and suffer hunger; But

they who seek the Lord shall not be in want of any good thing" (Psalm 34:10).

Peace – "The steadfast of mind You will keep in perfect peace, because he trusts in You" (Isaiah 26:3).

Help – "Cast your burden upon the Lord, and He will sustain you; He will never allow the righteous to be shaken" (Psalm 55:22).

Guidance – "I will instruct you and teach you in the way which you should go; I will counsel you with My eye upon you" (Psalm 32:8). "Your word is lamp to my feet, and a light to my path" (Psalm 119:105).

Anxiety/Worry – "... Casting all your anxiety on Him, because He cares for you" (1 Peter 5:7).

Comfort - "... the father of mercies and God of all comfort, who comforts us in all our afflictions..." (2 Corinthians 1:3).

God comforts us through His presence and Word. Is it any wonder that the psalmist tells us that God is a *very present help* in the time of trouble? I think not. The psalmist knows that God's Word is powerful and effective in all situations. The psalmist also knows that self-evaluation without the aid of God's Word can provide a false result. The psalmist may feel like a wine skin in the smoke, but these are his words about himself; they are not God's thoughts or words about him.

A prime example of the above point is the self-evaluation of ten of the twelve spies upon their return from spying out the promise land. They saw themselves as grasshoppers in the sight of the giants that were in the land. This was their self-evaluation of the situation, not God's.

So before we forget the impact that God's Word can have on us, and we evaluate the situation apart from God's Word, let us remember that God's Word is a powerful change agent. God's Word will change our self-concept. God's Word will change our perspective on life. God's Word will set us free and release us from the past. God's Word will provide comfort for us.

God's Word will let us know that even though we feel like a wineskin in the smoke, He will revive by His Word and loving kindness.

Lord, even though I know that I'm not to get caught up in the cares of life and expend my energy being anxious - I do. Sometimes I feel so useless and of no value. I just feel tired, ruined and burned out. Lord, would You help me? Would You let me see things through Your eyes and Word? Reaffirm in my heart and my mind that nothing is too difficult for You. I need Your help!

Psalm 143

1. Hear my prayer, O Lord,
   Give ear to my supplications!
   Answer me in Your faithfulness, in Your righteousness!

2. And do not enter into judgment with Your servant.
   For in Your sight no man living is righteous.

3. For the enemy has persecuted my soul;
   He has crushed my life to the ground;
   He has made me dwell in dark places, like
   those who have long been dead.

4. Therefore my spirit is overwhelmed within me;
   My heart is appalled within me.

5. I remember the days of old;
   I meditate on all Your doings;
   I muse on the work of Your hands.

6. I stretch out my hands to You;
   My soul longs for You, as a parched land.   Selah.

7. Answer me quickly, O Lord, my spirit fails;
   Do not hide Your face from me,
   Or I will become like those who go down to the pit.

8. Let me hear Your loving kindness in the morning;
   For I trust in You;
   Teach me the way in which I should walk;
   For to You I lift up my soul.

9. Deliver me, O Lord, from my enemies;
   I take refuge in You.

10. Teach me to do Your will,
    For You are my God;
    Let Your good Spirit lead me on level ground.

11. For the sake of Your name, O Lord, revive me.
    In Your righteousness bring my soul out of trouble.

12. And in Your loving kindness, cut off my enemies
    And destroy all those who afflict my soul,
    For I am Your servant.

Prayer

Hear my prayer, O Lord, Give ear to my supplications!
Answer me in Your faithfulness, in Your righteousness!
- Psalm 143:1

The people of God, no matter if they are Old Testament or New Testament saints, have always found themselves living in the interim between God's promises and the fulfillment of those promises. As New Testament saints we live in the interim between what shall be, or the then and there, and the reality of life in the present, or the here and now. The interim between the then and there and the here and now is filled with all kinds of problems, tensions and entailments called life.

It is in this present interim of tension, called life, which we, the people of promise, often find ourselves in need of help. We find ourselves in situations that need God's intervention to provide relief, resolve or, at least, the wherewithal to handle the tension.

The way we ask God to intervene into the arenas of our lives is by prayer. It is through prayer that we ask for guidance. It is by prayer that we ask for deliverance. It is through prayer that we ask for provision. It is by prayer that we ask for protection. Prayer is our direct line of communication to God to ask for His intervention into our lives.

Even though we, the people of promise, recognize we have access to the One who can make a difference in our lives, many times we don't know what or how to pray. This is where the Psalms can help us formulate our prayers for specific needs or be a template for our prayers.

One area that many of us often find ourselves is in need of guidance. The mental and physical tension of the situation before us has so clouded our vision that we just don't know what to do. We are in need of supernatural guidance. This is exactly the situation in which David finds himself. Psalm 143 is David's invitation to God to intervene and to make a difference in his life.

We do not know the exact cause of David's tension, but we do know that it was extreme and it was about to take its toll on him. In verse four of this Psalm, David tells us about the condition of his inner being. He says that his spirit is overwhelmed and his heart is appalled. In verse seven, he asks God to intervene quickly because his spirit is about to fail, and if God does not quickly intervene it will be over. In our vernacular, David is saying that he is at the end of his rope. I'm sure that we all have been there.

It is in this time of extreme tension and turmoil that David asks God to revive him, to bring his soul out of trouble, to cut off or silence his enemies, and to destroy all those who torment his soul. He also asks God for assurance and guidance. Let us take a closer look at David's prayer beginning in verse eight of this Psalm.

The first thing he asks for is protection during the night hours of sleep. He wants the assurance that during the hours of unconsciousness, the hours of sleep, that he can count on God's protection. The Message handles the first half of verse eight as follows, "If you wake me each morning with the sound of your loving voice, I'll go to sleep each night trusting in you ..." (Psalm 143:8, The Message). One does not have to be a rocket scientist to realize that one is not going to hear anything in the morning if one is not protected through the night. Nighttime, bed time, can be a scary time for many. And, if not scary, at least a time of mental anguish when all kinds of thoughts are generated and run wild through the corridors of our minds. Instead of the bed becoming a place of rest and rejuvenation, it becomes a place of torture and mental torment.

David had all this tension in his life. Tension that could provide the ingredients for a great nighttime mental movie of torment. So David asks for help. He asks God if he can just have the assurance that he will go to sleep each night wrapped in a comforting blanket of His presence and hear His voice in the morning. Such assurance is better than any sleeping pill or tranquilizer. Medicines wear off and their effect dissipates. God does not wear off and His abiding presence does not dissipate. It is that heart felt assurance that God will never leave us or forsake us that can bring us comfort. It is the peace that comes from knowing that Christ is dwelling in our hearts that can bring us rest. It is a rest that passes all understanding.

The second thing David asks God for is direction. He asks God to teach him the way that he should go, or as The Message says, "... Point out the road I must travel; I'm all ears, all eyes before you" (Psalm 143:8). In other words, You have my full attention just show me what I am to do and I will do it.

I believe David is saying I have tried everything I know to do to resolve this tension and it is not working so now I submit to Your guidance. David is saying that he is one hundred percent open to divine guidance in his life. David is saying just give me some insight to the plan You have for my life. David is asking God to let him know that even though he is in a dark time of his life, it is okay for he is where he is supposed to be.

Such knowledge of doing right and being in the right can bring assurance and peace. For example, let us assume that you know a farmer who has a pond on his property and in that pond are some great fish. The only problem is there are no trespassing and no fishing signs posted all around the farmer's property. Your desire to fish at the pond, however, overrides your knowledge of the prohibition. So you sneak onto the property and begin to fish. The whole time you are there, you are on the look-out for the farmer. Every little noise will quicken the pulse, and there will be no relief from alertness until you are off the property. You may catch some great fish, but you will not have the peace of mind and relaxation that fishing excursions usually provide. Why? Because you were some place you were not supposed to be.

Now let us look at the same example with just one variation. You know a farmer who has a pond on his property and in that pond are some great fish. The farmer has posted no trespassing and no fishing signs all around his property. However, you have a strong desire to fish in the farmer's pond. Instead of sneaking onto his property you go up to his house and ask him for permission to fish in his pond. You tell him you will be very careful to not disturb his crops and livestock. The farmer, in turn, gives you permission to fish for two hours. With such knowledge, you now go to the pond in peace. You are not extra sensitive to every movement and sound. You are not apprehensive that the farmer might show up unexpectedly. Why? Because even though the farmer's land is posted, you have permission to be there. You can relax and enjoy the experience because you have the knowledge that you did right and, as a result of your actions, you are in the right place.

When the fisherman relinquished his desire to fish to the farmer, the owner of the pond, his fishing experience was much more enjoyable. When we submit our ambitions and desires to God, the Sovereign One, our journey through life will be much more enjoyable. That is not to say there will not be times of tension and difficulty, but during those times we can at least have the peace and assurance that we are where we are supposed to be because we have submitted ourselves to His divine guidance.

The third thing David asks for is deliverance from his enemies. He asks God to give him relief from the very ones that have brought tension and difficulty into his life.

David's request tells us a couple of things about life. First, it tells us something that we all know, and that is, in life we are going to have problems. We are going to have problems even when we our serving God with all our heart. Second, it tells us that we can go to God with our problems and ask not only for assistance, but also deliverance. Strength to persevere and divine assistance are wonderful gifts, but if we are persevering it means the problem or difficulty is still present. Deliverance, on the other hand, means the problem has been removed or made ineffective. David is asking for deliverance.

David is not shopping around for assistance to resolve his dilemma. He makes it very clear that he has not chosen God as one of many options, but God is his only option. As The Message states, "... you're my only hope!" (Psalm 143:9)

So many times it seems that when we are faced with problems our response to God may be like David's, "You are my only hope." It means something totally different coming out of our mouths than it did coming out of David's mouth. To David it meant exactly what he said, "You are my only hope," first and foremost. Many times for us it means we have tried everything we know to do and God is the only option we have left. How much better off we would be if we were more like David. We should go to God first instead of Him being our last option to help in our dilemmas.

David is literally saying that he has hidden himself in the Lord. If David has hidden himself in the Lord, then he is concealed in the Lord. And if concealed in the Lord, then he is protected by the Lord. To attack David, the enemy would first have to defeat the Lord, and that is impossible. So by hiding in God, or concealing himself in God, or taking refuge in the Lord, David is secure in the mighty arms of God even while in the presence of the enemy.

The question for us when seeking relief from our enemies and problems of life is, how does one go about hiding or concealing himself or herself in God? The way we hide our self in God is by believing He is able and by putting complete trust in Him. In the heat of the battle, the application of the remedy for relief is, at times, difficult. We must remember, however, that He is not our last hope, but He is our only hope.

The fourth thing David is going to ask for is instruction on how to do His will. Again, I like the way The Message handles this request. It states, "Teach me how to live to please you..." (Psalm 143:10). To instruct or to teach someone something is to alter their behavior. Some would say that the true test for learning is if there has been a change in behavior. In other words, the degree of learning is in direct ratio to one's congruency to what has been taught. Look at what David is asking. David is asking God to mold him into a person that brings Him pleasure. David is saying, "I'm open to being shaped by You and for You, for I wish to bring You pleasure."

David has declared God as his Deity of allegiance. The One who has the final word in his life. Therefore he wants to please Him. And the way to please God is to learn His ways; to be molded into congruency to His will. So David says, "teach me how to please You."

I wonder if sometimes we have gotten this sequence reversed. We may choose God, but we want Him to please us instead of us pleasing Him. We may never say this out loud, but sometimes our attitudes and actions speak louder than our words. Often we think of God as a mail order catalog and that He is obligated to send us what we request. If He does not respond as we wish, our allegiance wanes. Our motto is we please Him as He pleases us.

This self-centered attitude seems to be completely foreign to David. His desire, in spite of his circumstances, is to bring pleasure to God. Such an attitude should be ours also. Why? Because He is our God and we should desire to bring Him pleasure.

I can assure you from a biblical perspective that whenever God's people desired to bring Him pleasure by living their lives after His declared ways, they were always the recipients of His blessings. I believe David knew this principle and we should not only know it but also practice it in our daily lives.

Finally, David is going to ask for a Spirit-lead life onto some cleared and level ground. I think this request is pregnant with desire.

First, David is acknowledging his need for God's direction in his life. David realizes that his life needs to be equipped with God's "GPS", so to speak. So, he is requesting that God's Spirit be his guide and compass. David realizes that self-guidance can many times lead to unpleasant situations that seem to be dead ended, but that a Spirit-directed life is never dead ended.

Second, David requests direction for his Spirit-lead life. He asks for cleared and level land. Cleared and level land represents three things. First, it represents freedom from labor. The trees, stumps, snags, rocks and brush have already been removed. The hard work of excavation has already been done. In David's day such work would have been much more difficult than in our day. Second, cleared land is ready to become productive either with crops or construction. Finally, cleared and level land is much more easily traveled and worked than hilly land.

I believe David is asking for three things when he asks to be led by the Spirit onto cleared and level land. He is asking for rest, productivity and effectiveness in service. These are commodities that would be beneficial in all our lives.

Why did David feel he had the right to ask God for these blessings? The answer is to be found in the last line of this Psalm. David felt confident in asking for these things because he declares himself to be a servant of God.

The Hebrew word used here for servant conveys the idea of one who is not in control of his destiny, but is under the control or power of another. So David is saying, "since I have voluntarily submitted my life to You, I am asking You to intervene in my life and make a difference." David's declaration that he is God's servant is much like his recognition that his times are in God's hand (Psalm 31:15). Because of this awareness and declaration David feels secure and confident in asking his Master for help in his time of tension.

Long before we ask for God's mighty arm to intervene in our circumstances we need to recognize our position before Him. We must voluntarily submit to His authority and power. He is the Master and we are the servants.

If we possessed the power to control and direct our lives then we would not be calling out to Him in the first place. We need to recognize and accept that our times are in His hands and rest in that truth. And, while resting in this truth, we need to remember that one of the benefits of being in God's hands is that ultimately God causes all things to work together for good to those who love God (Romans 8:28).

When this prayer is reduced down to its essence, David is asking God for five things. David is requesting assurance of God's continual presence, guidance in the path of life, protection from opposition, growth in his spiritual development, and rest from conflict. David is asking for assurance, guidance, protection, growth and rest.

These are five areas of our lives that at sometime, we will all need God's hand of intervention. Maybe one area is more needed than another depending on our current circumstances, but all five areas are needed at different times.

I would encourage you to pray this prayer often. Write it out and post it in different places within your house, in your car and at work. Pray it daily and in times of tension or need throughout the day and see that God is a *very present help*.

Lord, I'm going through some difficult times right now. I don't know how much more tightly the rubber band of my life can be wound before it breaks. So in my time of need, would You be a very present help and provide me with some assurance of Your presence, guidance of Your Spirit, protection by Your almighty power, growth in Your Word, and Your rest and peace that passes all understanding. Amen

Psalm 146

1. Praise the Lord!
   Praise the Lord, O my soul!

2. I will praise the Lord while I live;
   I will sing praises to my God while I have my being.

3. Do not trust in princes,
   In mortal man, in whom there is no salvation.

4. His spirit departs, he returns to the earth;
   In that very day his thoughts perish.

5. How blessed is he whose help is the God of Jacob,
   Whose hope is in the Lord his God,

6. Who made heaven and earth,
   The sea and all that is in them;
   Who keeps faith forever;

7. Who executes justice for the oppressed;
   Who gives food to the hungry.
   The Lord sets the prisoners free.

8. The Lord opens the eyes of the blind;
   The Lord raises up those who are bowed down;
   The Lord loves the righteous;

9. The Lord protects the strangers;
   He supports the fatherless and the widows,
   But He thwarts the way of the wicked.

10. The Lord will reign forever,
    Your God, O Zion, to all generations.
    Praise the Lord!

Help

Do not trust in princes, in mortal man, in whom there is no salvation.

- Psalm 146:3

At some point in our lives, all of us find ourselves in a situation where we need help. At such times of need, the issue becomes where should we turn for assistance and help? Sometimes the answer is obvious. Sometimes it is not. Sometimes the answer to where we turn for help is found in the nature of the problem. For example, if we have a flat tire, it is obvious that we need a tire repair shop, or if we have a broken tooth, we need to go to the dentist. But what if when we get to tire repair shop we are told we need a new tire and some major work done on the car's suspension? Or upon arrival at the dentist, he tells us we need a crown to fix the tooth and some other dental work done or we stand the chance of further complications. To make matters worse, we don't have the extra money. Where do we turn?

What if the problem is not the need for extra money? What if the problem is about things that don't have easy answers like flat tires and broken teeth? What if the problem is about marriage, or health, or family, or career? Where does one turn for help? Usually we look for help horizontally before we look vertically.

There seems to be a natural tendency in mankind to trust in man rather than to trust in God. It is as though it is easier to trust in what can be seen (man and his limited resources) than to trust in what cannot be seen (God and His infinite resources). The Scripture contains many examples of this practice. King Asa is a prime example of this habit. His story can be found in 2 Chronicles 14-16.

King Asa had been privileged to see the mighty hand of God many times in his life and reign as king. But when King Baahsa of Israel came against him, instead of trusting in God for help, as he had done in the past, he sought assistance from the King of Aram in Damascus. As a result of his actions, King Asa is told that because he trusted in the King of Aram for help instead of God that the army of Aram had escaped out of his hand. In other words, King Asa could have been delivered from the King of Israel and won a victory over the King of Aram if he had only trusted in God for help instead of man. King Asa is told that he acted foolishly in this matter.

To further illustrate this point, when King Asa became sick in his feet, instead of trusting in God for help, the Scripture tells us that he did not seek the Lord, but sought out physicians.

The Scripture also gives us many examples of others that trusted in men for help instead of trusting in God. The Scripture also warns against doing so. The psalmist says in Psalm 118:8-9 that, "It is better to take refuge in the Lord than to trust in man.

It is better to take refuge in the Lord than to trust in princes." In verse three of Psalm 146 we are instructed, "Do not trust in princes, in mortal man, in whom there is no salvation."

This whole idea of who we are to trust for help is summed up very nicely in Jeremiah 17:5-8. In verse five we are told that, "...Cursed is the man who trusts in mankind and makes flesh his strength..." In verse seven we are told that, "Blessed is the man who trusts in the Lord and whose trust is the Lord."

Psalm 146 is going to explain why we should trust in the Lord instead of man for help. According to verses three and four, we are told not to trust in man because he is not able to provide salvation. In other words, he is not able to rescue us and/or provide ultimate help for us. The reason being is he is in the same boat as us. He is not eternal. He is mortal. When man dies, his presence and influence are gone and he returns to dust. Therefore, help from man is temporal at best.

God, on the other hand, according to verse ten, differs from mortal man in that He is immortal. He is eternal. He reigns forever to all generations. He is ever-present, and, therefore, can provide help or salvation in all situations. And according to verse four, the person who recognizes this is blessed because he has placed his trust in the God of Israel for help. His hope is in the Lord and he will not be disappointed. Or as God says in Isaiah, "... No one who hopes in Me ever regrets it" (Isaiah 49:23, The Message).

In verses six through nine of this Psalm we are told how God differs from man. The psalmist is going to provide a list of God's qualities that should cause us to want to put our trust in God for help rather than man.

First, we are told that God made everything that was made. God is the CREATOR of all. This is a very important fact. It means that God is supreme. The Lord speaking says, "Thus says the Lord... the One who formed you from the womb, 'I, the Lord, am the maker of all things, stretching out the heavens by Myself, and spreading out the earth all alone'..." (Isaiah 44:24). Man has not done this. Man does not even understand how it was all done. This means God has no equal. He is God alone. If God created everything, then why seek out help from creation when we have access to the Creator? If God made it, then He understands how it all works. Because God is Creator, He is our supreme helper. He is our Creator!

Next, we are told that God never goes back on His Word or vacillates in regard to truth. He is FAITHFUL in all things. For most of us, this is a hard concept to grasp. Most of us know someone that has massaged his or her word at sometime in some situation. But that is not the case with God. He never alters His Word. In Psalm 119:89 we are informed that God's Word is settled or stands firm in heaven. If God said it, it is a done deal. So when we are told in Psalm 46:1 that God is our refuge and strength, a *very present help* in trouble, we can count on it as being the true and steadfast Word of God. Since God watches over His Word to perform it (Jeremiah.1:12), we can count on Him for help in the time of need. He is Faithful!

The third thing we are told about God is that He is a FAIR JUDGE in that he executes justice for the oppressed. Again, this is a difficult concept for us to conceive, particularly in today's push for political correctness. Today we are seeing the personal bias or agendas of judges overriding the will of the people. Today in our society one judge can override the vote of millions and bring into question the very moral fabric of our country and hold our government hostage to their political agenda.

The case for unfair judges is not only a reflection of our society. Throughout history the oppressed and the poor have been at the mercy of the court and usually on the short end of the stick. The people of means and influence have usually gotten the benefit of the doubt and received the favor of the court. Not so with God. He is a Fair Judge. As the apostle Peter reflects on what had transpired at Cornelius' house, he says in Acts 10:34, "...God is not one to show partiality...." The apostle Paul says in Romans 2:11, "For there is no partiality with God." Jew or Gentile, rich or poor, irrespective of social strata or power of influence, God treats us all the same. He is a Fair Judge. We can go to Him for help and expect fairness. He is a Fair Judge!

Next we are told that God is our PROVIDER in that he supplies the needs of the hungry. This is a truth that is attached to God from Genesis to Revelation. It was Abraham, when the ram was provided as a substitute for Isaac, that gave God the name Jehovah-Jireh, which means the Lord Will Provide. The apostle Paul, hundreds of years later, affirms for us that God can supply all our needs according to His riches in glory in Christ Jesus (Philippians 3:19). He is our Provider!

The psalmist next tells us that God sets the prisoner free. God is our EMANCIPATOR. An emancipator is one who releases one from bondage and oppression. This is exactly what God has done and is doing for mankind. When Jesus states His commission and mission in Luke 4:18-19, He specifically states that He has come for the purpose to proclaim release to the captives. As we know we were all captives of sin and oppressed by Satan. But by the work of Christ we have been set free from the bondage and oppression of the kingdom of darkness. The apostle Paul tells us in Colossians 1:13-14 that "...He rescued us from the domain of darkness and transferred us to the kingdom of His beloved Son, in whom we have redemption, the forgiveness of sins". By His life, death, resurrection and ascension, we who have confessed His name have experienced the eternal emancipation proclamation. We have been set free. He is our Emancipator!

Next, we are told that the Lord opens blind eyes. He is our ILLUMINATOR. Again, this is part of Jesus' commission and mission according to Luke 4:18-19. For, in this passage, we are told that part of His ministry was to restore sight to the blind. I believe that he is our Illuminator both spiritually and physically. The disciple John addresses this in his gospel.

In John chapter eight, Jesus presents a discourse about being the light of the world. He is saying that those that believe in Him and follow Him no longer have to walk in darkness, but can walk in light. In other words, those that align themselves with Him are no longer spiritually blind or relegated to stumbling around in the dark, but have the illumination of His presence to assist and guide them. Whereas we were once incarcerated in the kingdom of darkness, we have now been released and transferred to the kingdom of light. He is our spiritual Illuminator.

In John chapter nine, Jesus also shows us he is our physical Illuminator. In this chapter Jesus heals a man that has been physically blind from birth. It is like Jesus is presenting an object lesson. He is demonstrating physically what he came to do spiritually. Here is a man, who had never seen a ray of light, given his sight because he trusted in Jesus to be his Illuminator.

Think about this, a man who for all his life had walked in darkness was now walking in light. A blind man received sight because he had come in contact with the One who had come to restore sight to the blind. A man who proclaimed after meeting the Illuminator, "...though I was blind, now I see... He opened my eyes." According to the passage he saw both physically and spiritually.

This passage also tells us that this was the first time since the beginning of time that a person who was born blind had received their sight (John 9:32). The apostle John is not only making reference to the physical miracle but also to the fact that One had arrived on the stage of humanity that could release us from the kingdom of darkness and place us in the kingdom of light. The Illuminator has come and opened our eyes so that we can see the truth and the truth will set us free. Man can't do that. Only Jesus can. He is our Illuminator!

The psalmist now informs us that He rises up those who are bowed down. He is our COMFORTER. The psalmist tells us that God is the One who lifts our head (Psalm 3:3). In 2 Corinthians 1:3, God is referred to as, "... the God of all comfort." In the eleventh chapter of Matthew's gospel, Jesus instructs all those that are exhausted from the cares of life to come to Him and He will give them rest. He will comfort us. He is the ever-present Comforter for He has sent another like Himself in the presence of the Holy Spirit to stand beside us, to lead, guide and comfort. We are beneficiaries of His personalized comfort.

I could go on and on about God being our Comforter in all and every kind of situation. As a pastor I have seen His ability to comfort in hospital rooms, at funeral homes, upon hearing the worst of news, in the midst of tragedy, and in more situations than I can mention.

Just the mention of the name of Jesus brings comfort. Truly there is something about that Name. I don't know how many times the reading of a passage of Scripture has brought hope to a seemingly hopeless situation, or a simple prayer has brought peace in a tumultuous situation. But I do know that when we reflect on Him and ask for help, He is there to provide comfort physically, emotionally and spiritually. He is our Comforter!

The psalmist now tells us that the Lord loves the righteous. He is our REWARDER. It is true that God loves all mankind, but this verse seems to leave the impression that there is something extra special of God's love for the righteous; those that have aligned themselves to His ways. It only stands to reason that if God has extended His love to all mankind regardless if they have accepted or rejected the offering that there would be a strong outpouring of His love to those who have accepted His gift. I believe this fact is in harmony with the teachings of both the Old Testament and the New Testament.

A prime Old Testament example of this truth is found in Exodus 20:6, "...but showing loving kindness to thousands, to those who love Me and keep My commandments." An Old Testament verse I particularly like in relationship to this truth of God being our Rewarder is Psalm 16:11. This verse tells us that, "...In Your presence is fullness of joy; In Your right hand are pleasures forever." One is not going to be in His presence or in His right hand unless they have accepted His love and aligned themselves with His ways. The reward for such action is fullness of joy and pleasures forever. I will not even attempt to describe what "fullness of joy" and "pleasures forever" may mean, but I do believe these expressions do not speak of shortage but abundance, and not of temporal blessings but eternal rewards. He is our Rewarder.

The New Testament is full of teaching about the love of God directed toward mankind. Probably John 3:16 is the most notable. Another New Testament verse that speaks to the issue of God's special attention in dispatching His love and all that it entails to those that are righteous (not perfect) through faith in Christ is Romans 8:28. In this verse we are told that, "...God causes all things to work together for good to those who love God... ." In other words, those who have aligned themselves with God through faith in Jesus Christ can expect special intervention on their behalf from God. He is our Rewarder!

Another reason we can go to God for help is that He is our PRESERVER. The psalmist informs the reader that God protects the stranger and supports the fatherless and the widows. The stranger and the fatherless and the widows need help at times to maintain equilibrium in their lives.

A stranger has no apparent support system. You may be a stranger because you are among people you do not know. You may be a stranger because you have no friends or acquaintances available. Therefore, you do not know who to turn to for assistance and/or protection. And because you are a stranger, you may need protection. Even though you may be among many, you are all alone.

You may be a stranger because you are in new or unfamiliar surroundings. As a result of your current situation you are not sure what you should do or where you should go. You are in desperate need of guidance and direction. You need the assurance that someone is there to help. God is. God is our Preserver.

Many times in my travels I have experienced the emotions just described. Particularly when traveling internationally. I have felt the emotions of being a stranger among people of a different language, culture and ethnic backgrounds. I know the feeling of being in a situation of having no one to communicate with or to turn to for help because of language barriers. I know the emotions that can be generated from being a stranger in hostile situations. I know what it is like to stand in unfamiliar airports, cities and places not knowing exactly what to do. I know what it is like to be a stranger. But, I also know that in those situations when I have called out to God, He has always helped. I'm sure He has provided assistance and protection even when I have not specifically asked for it. God is our Preserver.

Not only does our Preserver protect the stranger, but He also supports, or relieves, the fatherless and the widows. In other words, He takes care of those that might have difficulties in supplying their own care and preservation. God cares about us no matter our situation. God is our Preserver!

The psalmist now tells us that God thwarts, or makes crooked, the way of the wicked. I like to think of this activity of God, as God is our TERMINATOR. In Psalm 147:6, we are told that He brings the wicked to the ground. And Isaiah tells us in the chapter 54 verse 17 that no weapon that is formed against you shall prosper. All throughout God's Word we see God terminating the plans of those that are against Him or His people.

A terminator is one who brings an end to an activity, or one who stops something from continuing. The psalmist and Isaiah are telling us that God stops the activity or plans of the wicked before they are completed. What a blessed assurance to know that God is at work terminating, bringing to an end, the plans of our opposition. The prophet Jeremiah tell us, "'For I know the plans that I have for you,' declares the Lord, 'plans for welfare and not for calamity to give you a future and a hope'" (Jeremiah 29:11). God is our Terminator!

This Psalm tells us that we are blessed if our hope and trust is in the Lord as opposed to trusting in other humans regardless of their social position. Let us never forget that God is our Creator, Faithful One, Fair Judge, Provider, Emancipator, Illuminator, Comforter, Rewarder, Preserver, and Terminator. And what He is, He will always be... not so with man.

Our God is a *very present help* in all kinds of circumstances. He is able to out-perform mortal man. As the apostle Paul says, He is able to do exceeding abundantly beyond all that we ask or think (Ephesians 3:20).

In light of who He is and what He can do, when we find ourselves in need of help, let us put our trust in God and all that He is. Let us rest assured that He is able to perform. And let us demonstrate that trust by joining the psalmist in praise to our God.

Praise the Lord! Praise the Lord, O my soul!
I will praise the Lord while I live;
I will sing praises to my God while
I have my being. Psalm 146:1-2

Psalm 27

1. The Lord is my light and my salvation;
   Whom shall I fear?
   The Lord is the defense of my life;
   Whom shall I dread?

2. When evildoers came upon me to devour my flesh,
   My adversaries and my enemies, they stumbled and fell.

3. Though a host encamp against me,
   My heart will not fear;
   Though war arise against me,
   In spite of this I shall be confident.

4. One thing I have asked from the Lord, that I shall seek;
   That I may dwell in the house of the Lord
   All the days of my life,
   To behold the beauty of the Lord
   And to meditate in His temple.

5. For in the day of trouble He will conceal
   me in His tabernacle;
   In the secret place of His tent He will hide me;
   He will lift me upon a rock.

6. And now my head will be lifted up above
   my enemies around me,
   And I will offer in His tent sacrifices with shouts of joy;
   I will sing, yes, I will sing praises to the Lord.

7. Hear, O Lord, when I cry with my voice,
   And be gracious to me and answer me.

8. When You said, "Seek My face," my heart said to You,
"Your face, O Lord, I shall seek."

9. Do not hide Your face from me,
Do not turn Your servant away in anger;
You have been my help;
Do not abandon me nor forsake me,
O God of my salvation!

10. For my father and my mother have forsaken me,
But the Lord will take me up.

11. Teach me Your way, O Lord,
And Lead me in a level path because of my foes,

12. Do not deliver me over to the desires of my adversaries,
For false witnesses have risen against me,
And such as breathe out violence.

13. I would have despaired unless I had
believed that I would see the goodness of the Lord
In the land of the living.

14. Wait for the Lord;
Be strong and let your heart take courage;
Yes, wait for the Lord.

Fear

The Lord is my light and my salvation;
Whom shall I fear?
Psalm 27:1

When describing frightening situations that I had been in, I used to say, "I was ascared." My wife informed me that "ascared" was not a word. She told me I was either afraid or scared. I used to say to her, "Honey, if you had been where I was, you would have been ascared too."

Regardless of how we describe it, all of us have been afraid or scared at sometime in or life. Most of the time, fear is experienced when there is a threat of loss or the status quo is about to be altered. It may be the potential threat of loss of job, health, financial security, life or anything that is about to be taken unwillingly from us. All of these scenarios produce some degree of fear – threat of loss.

In Psalm 27 David supplies a remedy for fear. He tells us that complete trust in God is the antidote to fear. Look what he says in the first three verses of this Psalm.

> The Lord is my light and my salvation; Whom shall I fear? The Lord is the defense of my life; Whom shall I dread? When evildoers come upon me to devour my flesh, my adversaries and my enemies, they stumbled and fell. Though a host encamp against me, my heart will not fear; though war arise against me, in spite of this I shall be confident. Psalm 27: 1-3

David lists some dreadful things in these verses that are a threat to the status quo of his life. He says that even if the possibility of loss of life exists that he will not be afraid. And even if the threat of war exists he will not be fearful. Why? He says because the Lord is the defense of his life. I like the way The Message handles verse one of this Psalm.

> "Light, space, zest – that's God! So, with him on my side I'm fearless, afraid of no one and nothing."
> (Psalm 27:1, The Message)

So David's antidote for fear is complete confidence and trust in the Lord. David's fearless trust in the Lord was a trait that he had learned. David had been in life-threatening situations before (on the job and in war) and the Lord had delivered him. David tells King Saul in 1 Samuel 17:37, that the Lord had delivered him from the paw of the lion and the paw of the bear and that the Lord would deliver him from the hand of Goliath. God also protected him many times from the threatening hand of Saul. These were protective experiences that were logged in the heart and mind of David. David knew that it was because of God's hand upon his life that he had been successful and spared in these threatening situations.

David not only gained experiential knowledge of God that allowed him to trust God without fear, but he desired to nurture his relationship with God. We are told in verse four of this Psalm that David desired to dwell in God's house. This desire was not a causal wish but we are told that he was going to engage himself with effort to see that his desire was fulfilled. He was going to seek to dwell in His house, behold His beauty and to meditate or study at His feet.

The word "seek" means to search out, strive after, ask or beg. In essence, David is saying I will do everything that is within my power to dwell in His house, behold His beauty and to meditate or study at His feet.

David does not just want to visit for a few days or simply drop by for a visit, but he wants to dwell, remain or settle down in God's house. He wants to become a permanent resident. The best way to really get to know someone is to live with them. To live with someone is to learn their ways, how they think and how they react to different situations. To live with someone is to really get to know them. David says I really want to get to know more about God. I really want to learn His ways, how he thinks and how he responds. I want this privilege so badly that I will do all that is within my power to secure it.

Once David has observed the ways of the Lord from living in His house and sees that His ways are beautiful, he says that he will gaze upon His delightfulness. He goes on to say that he will contemplate with pleasure all that he has seen by being a permanent resident in God's presence.

As a result of all that he has seen, he is confident that in the day of trouble, in the day that he should be consumed with fear, that God will conceal him and take care of him. As a result of interfacing with God, David need not dread anything and is convinced that his heart should not vacillate with fear.

Look at what David says. He is convinced that in the day in which he is threatened by potential loss, he will not fear, because God will hide him in the secret place of His tent. A secret place is a place of ultimate protection because no one knows where it is. It is a secret place. David knew he could rely on the on the fact that in the day of potential loss, he was sheltered in God's mighty arms.

Look what else David has learned from dwelling in God's house. He is confident that in the day of threatened loss that God will lift him up on a rock so his head (his life) will be above his enemies. I believe David took this example of God's protective ways from his experience as a shepherd boy. As David would be tending his sheep a predator would come at one of the sheep. David would pick the sheep up and place it upon a high rock out of the way of danger, and now the battle was between David and the predator. I believe David saw God who he gazed upon as the Chief and Good Shepherd. In fact David tells us that the Lord is his Shepherd. God, the Shepherd, is the one who picks him up and places him out of the reach of the enemy who threatens and the conflict becomes the Lord's.

What is David's response to all of these blessings? He sings praise to God. Or, as The Message records, "... Already I'm singing God-songs; I'm making music to God" (Psalm 27:6).

What is David's final conclusion? He says in verse fourteen that we are to:

"Wait for the Lord;

Be strong and let your heart take courage;

Yes, wait for the Lord."

David is telling us to look and wait patiently for the Lord. Do not get ahead of what God is doing. Trust Him with all your heart. Trust in God is the antidote to fear.

The benefits of trusting and dwelling in God's presence are presented in many Psalms. For example Psalm 91 presents some of the benefits of dwelling in God's presence. Those that dwell in God's presence can expect God to be a place of refuge, a fortress, a protector, a shield, and a bulwark. Those that have made the Lord their refuge by trusting in Him need not be afraid or live in fear of aggressive action. Why? Because He is our refuge and He has put us under the protective care of His angels. Why has God done this? The psalmist says, because we have loved Him. As a result of our love and our trust in Him, we are assured that we will see His salvation. These are reassuring blessings and benefits for those who dwell in God's presence.

David informs us in Psalm 15 who may dwell in God's presence. David begins this Psalm by asking a question in verse one. He asks, "... who may abide in Your tent?" He then answers the question in verses 2-5a.

verse 2 – "He who walks with integrity, and works righteousness, and speaks truth in his heart."

verse 3 – "He does not slander with his tongue, nor does evil to his neighbor, nor takes up a reproach against a friend;"

verse 4 – "In whose eyes a reprobate is despised, but who

honors those who fear the Lord; he swears to his own hurt, and does not change;"

verse 5 – "He does not put out his money at interest, nor does he take a bribe against the innocent."

In the last sentence of this Psalm he says, "He who does these things will never be shaken" (Psalm 15:5b).

Trust in God in all situations is our security and our antidote to fear. Remember, if it was right to begin with God, then it is right to stay with God, or as The Message says, "Stay with God! Take heart. Don't quit. I'll say it again; stay with God" (Psalm 27:14).

"... *God, you're my refuge. I trust in you and I'm safe!*"
Psalm 91:2, The Message

Psalm 9:9-14

9. The Lord also will be a stronghold for the oppressed,
   A stronghold in times of trouble,

10. And those who know Your name will put their trust in You,
    For You, O Lord, have not forsaken those who seek You.

11. Sing praises to the Lord, who dwells in Zion;
    Declare among the peoples His deeds.

12. For He who requires blood remembers them;
    He does not forget the cry of the afflicted.

13. Be gracious to me, O Lord;
    See my affliction from those who hate me,
    You who lift me up from the gates of death,

14. That I may tell of all Your praises,
    That in the gates of the daughter of Zion
    I may rejoice in Your salvation.

Assurance

And those who know Your name will put their trust in You;
For You, O Lord, have not forsaken those who seek You.
- Psalm 9:10

In antiquity, an individual's name was often chosen to reflect some characteristic or trait. For example, Esau's name means red and hairy. Jacob's name means heel hanger, supplanter and deceiver. Daniel's name means God is my judge and Jesus' name Immanuel means God with us.

Just as an individual's name in the Scripture was often an indication of their character or some particular quality, so, too, God has revealed different aspects of His being and the different relationships He has with His creation by His names.

One name for God would be inadequate to express His greatness, because one name would not be able to present the many marvelous facets of His being. So the Old Testament contains a number of names and compound names for God which reveal a particular aspect of His character and dealings with mankind.

Since God has revealed Himself through His names, according to Psalm 9:10, the more we know and learn of His names the more we can rely on Him, and the more intimate our knowledge of God the more we are going to trust Him.

The verb –know – in this verse means knowledge gained from the senses or experience. In other words, those that have first hand knowledge of His name will put their trust in Him. Those who have interacted with Him will rely on Him.

As a result of our intimate or first hand knowledge of God, we can have the assurance that He will never leave or abandoned anyone who has put their trust in Him.

David, the author of this Psalm, is speaking from personal experience. He is not just sitting in his house and writing nice things about God. He knows what he was talking about. David is writing from personal knowledge and experience with God's names. David had put his trust in God's names many times. For example, in 1 Samuel 17 when David was confronting Goliath, he said that he was coming to confront him in battle in the name of the Lord of Hosts (17:45).

David is saying, "I come to You in the name Jehovah Sabaoth." The name Jehovah Sabaoth means the Lord who is in command and is in leadership of all created agencies and forces. Thus He is in command of all the angel armies. And we have already learned from Psalm 91 that God has charged His angels with our protection. David could proceed in confidence because he knew and put his trust in God's name, "Jehovah Sabaoth." The name speaks of God's great power to dispatch any assistance needed.

The Scripture tells us in Proverbs 18:10 that the name of

the Lord is a strong tower, and the righteous run into it and are saved. In other words, God's name is a source of security. In Scripture, the name Jehovah is translated Lord. Jehovah is the coming down, covenant keeping, eternal and redeeming God. And He is a strong tower. His name is a place of help, protection, provisions and security.

Jehovah is the name that is used for God when He reveals Himself in a covenant eternal way, or as a special help in the time of need. It is the name that speaks of Him being a very present help in every and all situations. Jehovah is the ever-present and unchanging One. In Scripture, sometimes the Jehovah name for God is joined with other words to form compound names for the Lord that represent specific areas that He is a definite help in the time of need. For example:

Jehovah-jireh   the Lord provides or sees. This name is found in Genesis 22:14. It is the account of God providing a ram for a sacrifice in place of Isaac.

Jehovah-rophe   the Lord that heals or the Lord your healer. This name was given to Israel in Exodus 15:25 as a promise that if they would keep God's commandments they would not be susceptible to the disease of Egyptians.

Jehovah-nissi   the Lord is my banner or rallying point. This name is found in Exodus 17:15. The name was given to God by Moses as a response to his God-given victory over Amalek.

Jehovah-shalom   the Lord is peace. This name was given to God by Gideon in Judges 6:24 after the angel of the Lord appeared to him and told him to deliver Israel from the Midianites.

Jehovah-rohi   the Lord is my shepherd. This name is found in Psalm 23 and speaks of God and of the all-nurturing, caring, leading and protecting character of God.

Jehovah-tsidkenu   the Lord is our righteousness. This name is in Jeremiah 23:5-6 and is prophecy about one who is to come and speaks to the fact that in all His dealings He will be and act righteous.

Jehovah-shammah   the Lord is there, or present. This name is found in Ezekiel 48:35 and is saying that the name of the eternal city shall be the Lord is there.

We have seen, in these compound Jehovah names, God revealing Himself as a very present help or source of encouragement. We have seen that the Lord sees and provides. He is also our healer and rallying point in good and bad times. He is our Peace in times of tension and is capable of providing all our needs as our Shepherd. Unlike man, He will always deal with us in fairness and righteousness. And God is ever-present with us. He will never leave or forsake us.

No wonder Paul tells the Philippians that his desire is to "know" Him, because, as the psalmist said, to "know" Him is to trust Him and God has not forsaken anyone who desires to know Him. He is a very present help in trouble!

Lord, help me and teach me more about You so that I can know You in a fuller way and therefore trust You in all circumstances that I encounter.

Final Thoughts

All of us need assistance or help at sometime in our lives. Usually when we need help, something is about to change or has changed from the status quo. It may be a change in our finances, marriage, job, health and the list goes on.

The psalmist calls these changes, detours in our lives. He calls these detours the valley of the shadow of death or the valley of deep darkness. This valley of deep darkness can be any situation that brings gloom, sorrow, sadness, distress, extreme disappointment or loss. It can be any situation that detours us from the peaceful and normal. In such situations, help beyond our resources is needed.

As followers of the Almighty, much of the time, if not all of the time, we think we should live and travel only on easy or peaceful streets. Yet the reality is as long as we live in a fallen world, we are going to be occasionally detoured onto trouble and hardship avenues. Jesus tells us in Matthew 6:34 that, "... Each day has enough trouble of its own." And in John 16:33 Jesus tells us, "... In the world you have tribulation, but take courage; I have overcome the world." In other words, there are going to be detours in life, but help is available in Him.

When on one of these detours I want you to remember one thing. All detours ultimately lead back to the main road. What is the main road? God and His Word. When everything around you is changing remember that God and His Word are not. They are permanent.

Remember:

"Jesus Christ is the same yesterday and today and forever."

Hebrews 13:8

"For I, the Lord, do not change..."

Malachi 3:6

"For the grass withers, the flower fades, but the word of God stands forever."

Isaiah 40:8

"Forever, O Lord, Your word is settled in heaven."

Psalm 119:89

Let us never forget that when everything is changing around us we can be assured of this one fact, God and His Word are not. God and His Word are permanent. And that is what makes these Psalms that we have looked at in the previous chapters such a valuable help in the time of need. No matter if we are on easy or peaceful streets or we find ourselves detoured onto trouble or hardship avenues God and His Word are the same. He is a very present help.

Final Thoughts

My prayer for you is — Psalm 20

1. May the Lord answer you in the day of trouble! May the name of the God of Jacob set you securely on high!

2. May He send you help from the sanctuary, and support you from Zion!

3. May He remember all your meal offerings, and find your burnt offerings acceptable!   Selah.

4. May He grant you your heart's desire and fulfill all your counsel!

5. We will sing for joy over your victory, and in the name of our God we will set up our banners. May the Lord fulfill all your petitions.

6. Now I know that the Lord saves His anointed; He will answer him from His holy heaven, with the saving strength of His right hand.

7. Some boast in chariots and some in horses, but we will boast in the name of the Lord, our God.

8. They have bowed down and fallen, but we have risen and stood upright.

9. Save, O Lord, may the King answer us in the day we call.

Summary

This book is the result of years of integrating life's experiences with the Psalms.

I have found the message of the Psalms to be very comforting in a variety of situations. In this book I have shared select Psalms that have been a very present help to me as I have struggled with life's difficulties. I trust they will likewise minister to you.

Ken is a seasoned minister who has experience in all facets of church ministry and pastoral leadership. He has been instrumental in the training of church leaders and pastors as well as ministering at churches, seminars, camps, retreats, and conferences nationally and internationally.

He holds a BA from Vanguard University and a D.Min. from California Graduate School of Theology.

He and his wife, Lyn, live in Phoenix, Arizona and he is currently traveling as a minister to the church worldwide.